# DOVETAILS

## The Hand Tool Approach

MITCH PEACOCK

# DOVETAILS

## The Hand Tool Approach

# CONTENTS

# FOREWORD

I have been a professional furniture maker for over 25 years, and during that time I have made my fair share of dovetails. In the beginning I tried every method to create dovetails. I used the band saw, the table saw, countless jigs, and routers. In the end I settled on hand cut.

Mitch's book *Dovetails – The Hand-Tool Approach* is one of the most comprehensive and thorough books available on the subject. It gives over two dozen types of dovetail, and various ways to achieve them. Whether this is your first attempt at woodworking, or if you are a seasoned veteran, this book has something for everyone.

These days we have computers, software and AI, but Mitch Peacock teaches you the one thing that technology can't: how to be a true craftsman.

My mentor, Dennis Laney, a professional woodworker of over 60 years, once told me: 'If a book has one new lesson to teach you it is worth its value.' Well, *Dovetails – The Hand-Tool Approach* teaches a multitude of lessons and in my opinion is worth its weight in gold.

Chad Stanton

Dovetail box with a curved side, made from a piece of firewood.

*An old crooked man*
*Keen saw and chisel cutting,*
*tight joint. Happy man.*

# INTRODUCTION

Dovetail joints have been in use for millennia, in boats, buildings and furniture, and to this day are often used, unfairly in my mind, to gauge the skill of woodworkers. With some instruction, practice and patience, I believe any woodworker is capable of smart dovetails.

After teaching joint preparation for a decade, both in person to classes and individuals and online through videos, I have developed well explained and carefully illustrated methods for preparing 28 types of widely used, decorative and puzzling dovetail joints, and have collected and developed my own techniques to greatly aid the learning and preparation process. You may well ask if you will ever need to use all these different joints, and the answer is almost certainly not – I haven't, but challenging myself to at least try them has undoubtedly improved my layout and hand-tool skills, making me a better woodworker.

## HOW TO USE THIS BOOK

It may seem as if this is just a reference book on the preparation of dovetail joints, and it can certainly be used as such – however, it can also be a learning journey in joinery layout and execution.

Seasoned woodworkers are likely to discover new techniques if they take the time to read Chapter 2, which covers those techniques that I have found either personally useful or useful for some of my students, before dipping into the dovetails they haven't encountered previously in the joint preparation chapters, 3 to 5.

Beginners and less experienced woodworkers are those who will benefit most from reading Chapter 1, in which the nomenclature of dovetailing is discussed so that we know what we're talking about, and then material choices, and suggestions are made on building a dovetailing tool kit, including ideas for workshop-made tools and jigs; then Chapter 2 on useful techniques. They should attempt all the first joints, covered in Chapter 3 in order, familiarising themselves with the basic steps and referring back to the techniques previously covered as required.

I have selected the joints presented in Chapter 3 to ease the beginner in steadily, and to introduce the most recognisable ones that many students initially seek to learn. Chapter 4 is dedicated to corner joints specifically, and Chapter 5 to an array of miscellaneous dovetail uses.

To avoid excessive repetition as each joint is presented, the preparation details included will build on those given in previous joints where appropriate – and occasionally a blind alley will be navigated for variety. If you are ever unclear as to the next step you should take, or the technique you should or could use, refer back to a simpler yet similar joint, where you will likely find the answer.

No discussion on dovetail joints should end without reference to some of the challenging puzzle joints that employ them. Chapter 6 includes four dovetail puzzle joints, and expect their preparation to be a study in accuracy to produce the greatest effect.

Whilst you now have all the information you need to prepare dovetails, you will also need to practise, and so as an incentive for yourself, or as appeasement for a partner losing you to the workshop, I have included, as Chapter 7, instructions and plans for making a gorgeous dovetailed box, suitable for a watch or a ring, and either cuff links or earrings. Consider it your first dovetailing apprentice piece.

Enjoy your dovetail journey – and remember, plaid shirts and jeans are not essential, but sharp tools are.

CHAPTER 1

# GETTING STARTED

Whilst woodworking is hardly rocket science, success and satisfaction are founded on good preparation. When preparing joints, accuracy at removing waste whilst retaining all else intact is the key, and knowing what material is waste comes down to clear and precise marking out. However, before marking out, the basic joint type needs to be chosen and tailored to its situation, including the properties of the wood species being used. This chapter will provide you with the required preparation to tackle the dovetail joints in this book, assuming you are not a complete stranger to basic woodworking.

Take the time to learn or refresh your knowledge of the terms used in dovetailing, and the main dovetail joints you are likely to encounter.

If you are already a woodworker you probably have sufficient tools to get started, but there are some specific ones that make work easier and more pleasurable, and as a result often more accurate. Those new to woodworking will be pleased to see how few tools will get you started, and how simple they are to use. Try building the shop-made tools shown, which can easily be a match for commercially available alternatives.

## DOVETAIL JOINT NOMENCLATURE

An understanding of the terms used in dovetailing is essential for a clear discussion on the topic while studying the joints described in this and other references; it will also stand you in good stead when talking with furniture designers, architects and woodworkers alike. There are regional variations as well as variations between hand-cut and machine-cut dovetails, amongst others, and the following includes many of those in addition to the standard terms used throughout this book.

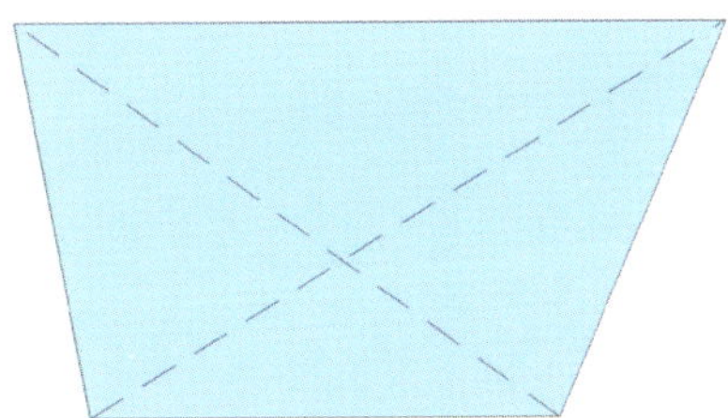

The trapezoid is the defining shape of a dovetail. *Left to right:* trapezoid, isosceles trapezoid, and overlaid on a through dovetail.

Hopper to feed millstones in a watermill. Before plywood and cheap nails, the sides of hoppers could be joined together with double-bevel dovetails.

## Dovetail

'Dovetail' is the defining shape found within a dovetail joint. It is known in geometry as a trapezoid (a quadrilateral with one pair of parallel sides), and most commonly an isosceles trapezoid, where the non-parallel sides are of equal length. Variations abound, for practical and aesthetic reasons, but the general shape will always be present.

## Dovetail Corner Joints

A dovetail corner joint is an angled joint between two boards, in their width (across the grain), using dovetail-shaped protrusions (pins and tails) and recesses (sockets). Most commonly the angle of the joint will be 90 degrees.

The main terms used with dovetail joints are listed in the table opposite.

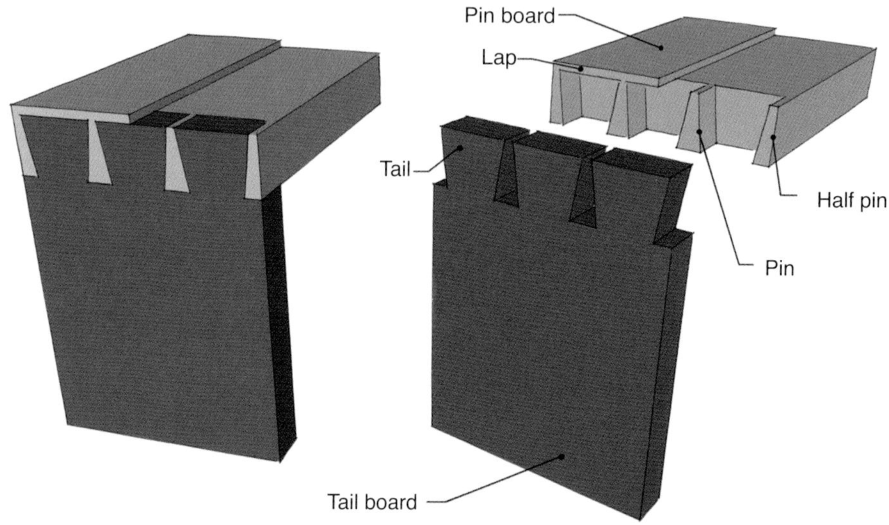


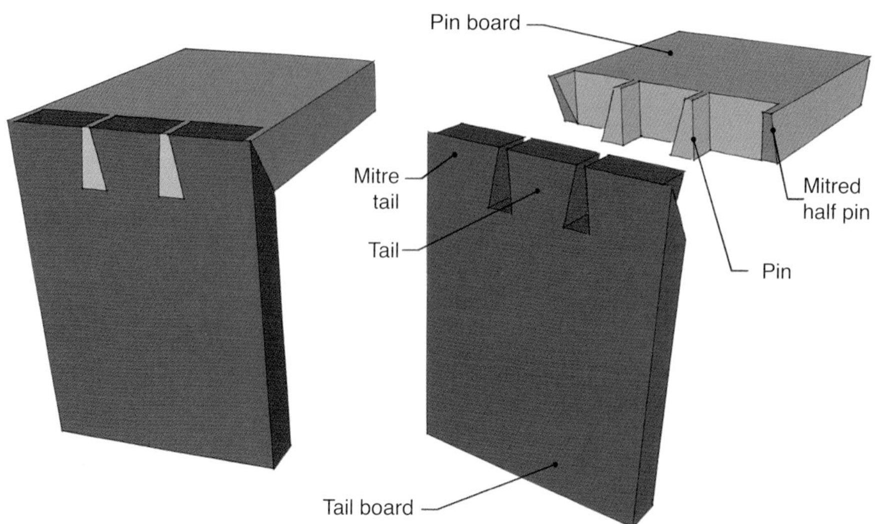


Hybrid of lapped and through dovetails (top) and mitre dovetail (bottom), showing the names for the most common parts.

| Main Terms Used When Describing a Dovetail Joint | |
|---|---|
| Tail | Name for the individual dovetail-shaped protrusions in hand-cut joints. A mitre tail retains some of what would normally be waste material, cut at an angle such that the two joining boards meet at a mitre joint. |
| Pin | Name for the remaining material between dovetail-shaped sockets in hand-cut joints. Confusingly it is also the name for all individual dovetail-shaped protrusions in machine-cut dovetails. A mitred pin has extra material cut away in order to form a mitre joint between itself and two adjacent mitre tails in the middle of a joint. |
| Half-pin | Name for the remaining material between extreme sockets and board edges in hand-cut joints. A mitred half-pin has extra material cut away in order to form a mitre joint between itself and a mitre tail at the edge of a tail board. |
| Rake | A measure of the slope that the side of a tail (or pin) takes, with respect to a centre line through that tail (or pin). It is normally given as a ratio when hand cut, or in degrees when machine cut. It is also referred to as the slope or angle. 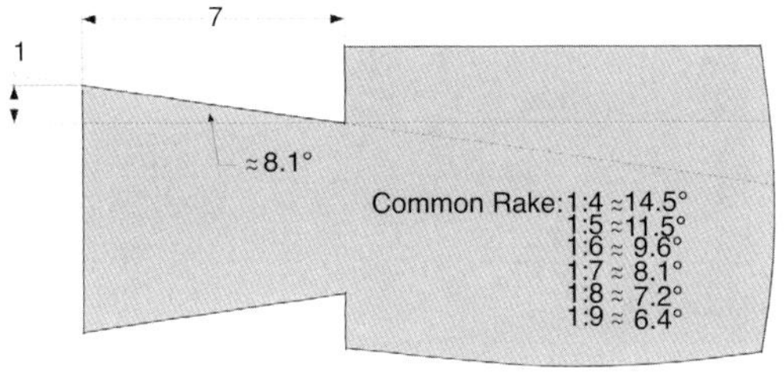<br><br>Measurement of rake, and common dovetail angle equivalents. |
| Pitch | Spacing between the centre lines of consecutive hand-cut tails, or machine-cut pins, where the spacing is equal across the whole joint. 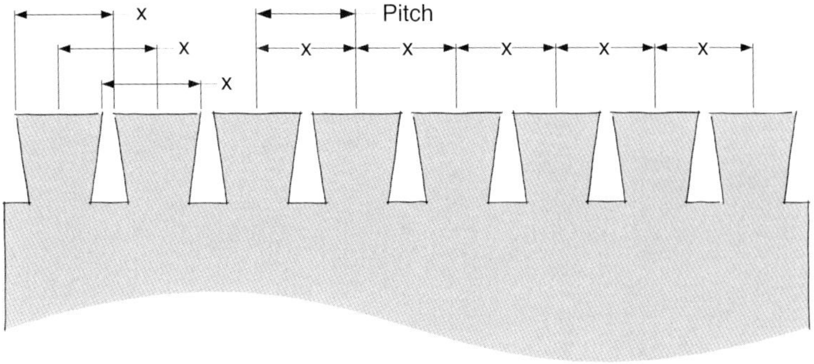<br><br>Pitch, when used to describe even spacing, is the distance between the centre lines of adjacent tails. For identical-sized tails, the pitch can be measured from side to consecutive side.<br>Historically, machine-cut joints were predominantly equally spaced, whereas the spacing of hand-cut joints was at the whim of the designer or craftsman. Very occasionally, pitch is incorrectly used in place of rake. So you may see 'pitch equals one in seven', which means that the rake is 1:7. |
| Lap | Solid face, covering the end grain of tails and/or pins. The distance by which the sockets, or tails, are held back from the front face. |

## DOVETAIL CORNER JOINTS

**Through Dovetails**

Pins and tails extend through the joining parts, remaining visible.

**Lapped (half-blind) Dovetails**

Single face overlaps and conceals the joint.

**Mitre Dovetails**

Edges are mitred rather than butted together.

**Secret (blind lap) Dovetails**

Both faces overlap to conceal the joint.

**Secret Mitre (full-blind) Dovetails**

Mitre dovetail with laps that appears as a simple mitre joint.

**Bevelled (sloped) Dovetails**

One of the parts is canted over.

**Double Bevel (oblique, compound angled) Dovetails**

Both parts are canted over.

Dovetail corner joints usually connect boards at right angles to each other. Differences are mainly down to visibility of tails and pins, edge of corner treatment, corner of edges treatment, and tilt of boards from vertical.

Decorative variations of dovetail corner joints are possible, for aesthetic value and to further demonstrate a craftsman's skills. Usually these rely on simple changes to the tail and pin forms that are not too complicated to cut, and don't substantially weaken the joint.

Of course, all these corner joints can be prepared at non 90-degree angles, forming acute or obtuse versions of them.

### Other Dovetail Joints

Aside from the corner joints just described, dovetails are significant in other joints, the preparation of many of which will also be covered later in the book. As with the corner joints, it is the wedge shape of the tail together with the complementary shape of the socket that resists these other joints pulling apart.

A number of these joints can take on various forms, some of which will be described when the joints are prepared.

In addition it is worth noting that the dovetail can be combined with any number of other joints, and can be used in many different applications; however, this book is limited to a broad selection demonstrating its wide versatility.

## FURTHER DOVETAIL JOINTS

**Dovetail Halving**

Halving joint in which one or both of the usual parallel sides are angled to a dovetail.

**Dovetail Bridle**

Bridle joint with dovetail shaped tenons.

**Dovetail Tenon**

Dovetail tenon enters through a clearance mortise, then slides into a dovetailed mortise.

**Dovetail Mitre**

Mitred joint, such as a frame, that is reinforced by a dovetail tenon

**Dovetail Housing (slot/slip/ sliding dovetail)**

Undercut housing, into which a dovetail edge is inserted.

**Rising Dovetail**

Tapered dovetail for a tee connection, assembled on a diagonal.

**Carcass Dovetail (leg and rail)**

Holds rails to frames or panels with attached legs or corner posts, in the construction of a carcass.

**Dovetail Keys (bow-ties)**

Back-to-back tails, used to hold pieces together.

Other dovetail joints use the shape of the tail and socket to provide mechanical resistance to being pulled apart. These are some of the more common or notable occurrences.

## Puzzle Joints

The limited freedom of movement of dovetailed parts has spawned a number of illusions, or puzzles, of which I have included a few, if only for amusement.

For the illusion to work convincingly, each of these joints needs to be prepared well. Tight joint lines and flush surfaces hide what is really going on.

Three of the four puzzle dovetails that I have included in the book are true joints, and one is a trick. Before you reach the instructions on how to make them, see if you can guess which is the odd one out.

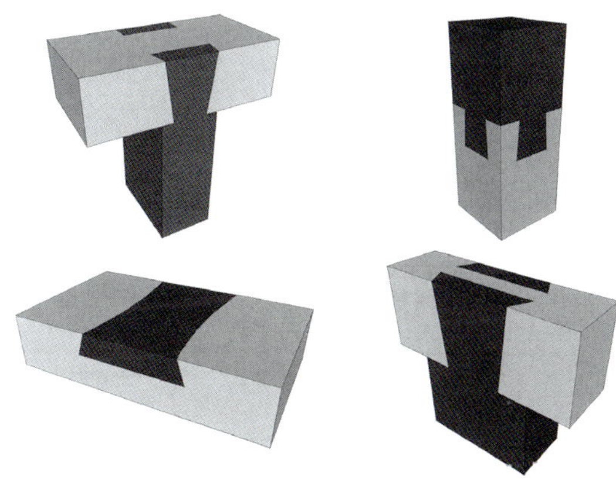

Puzzle dovetails appear impossible to assemble at first sight, yet they are remarkably simple once you know how. (*Clockwise from top left:* Impossible bridle, crossed double dovetail, twin rising dovetail, triple dovetail.)

### Carpenter or Cabinet Maker Dovetails?

Joints made by a carpenter (or more accurately a joiner) must be sound, quick to prepare, and should compromise the strength of components as little as possible. Their appearance is secondary, since they are often covered by such things as trim or paint. As such they are simply sawn and chopped, with pins and tails of roughly equal width.

Cabinet makers prepare show joints with precise layout and meticulous preparation, with an emphasis on final appearance rather than speed. The strength of the components need only fit their purpose, and as such, the layout of pins and tails is usually to minimise the amount of end grain on show, or to maximise contrast.

Both trades show, albeit in different ways, a great degree of skill in preparing exactly what is required for the purpose.

## MATERIALS

As woodworkers we have limited our dovetail material to just wood – at least in theory – but with approaching 100,000 species of trees on the planet, we still have plenty to choose from. I've yet to encounter a wood that can't be dovetailed, although some are certainly easier to work with than others, and some perform better to produce rigid and lasting joints. Start practising with the species that are moderately easy to work and in the cheaper price bracket while you learn the joint forms and the preparation process.

Although I shall concentrate on wood, beyond that, metals, plastics, composites – in fact any material that can be cut, cast or formed – can be used for dovetails. Of course, as with wood, individual materials have properties that will affect a joint's integrity, as might the orientation of a material's fibres, layers, crystal lattice, and so on. If in doubt, try it. Also,

Cabinet makers design dovetails for looks, minimising the pin size to reduce the end grain showing, whereas carpenters or joiners leave thick pins to retain strength, often covering up the joint later.

mixing wood with other materials can open up a host of opportunities, and modern adhesives such as epoxy resins can produce strong bonds between many dissimilar materials.

## Wood

Other than avoiding very hard and brittle woods, such as wenge, rosewood and ebony, when starting out I would encourage practising on anything available: it's all good experience.

There are some common woods that will prove more compliant and pleasurable to work with, and starting with any of these would be a sensible idea. Below are some woods from around the world which should help you find something reasonably local to try. Consider choosing contrasting woods while you practise, to highlight the joints and help you to gauge your progress.

### Green, Air-Dried or Kiln-Dried?

Given the choice I would opt to use air-dried wood for all dovetail work except large outdoor structures, where green (unseasoned) wood is particularly enjoyable to work with. Air-dried wood saws and chops reliably, and when re-sawn is less liable to large movement. Kiln-dried wood I try to avoid as much as possible, as I find prepared boards exhibit a hardened surface that is tougher to saw and chop through, two essential operations when dovetailing.

Kiln-dried wood should have similar workability to air-dried when both have the same moisture content, and my preference for air-dried is most likely due to experiencing too much wood that has been poorly kiln dried.

Both air-dried and kiln-dried wood should be left to settle to their intended environment

Some woods are easier than others when preparing dovetails for the first time. Start your dovetailing journey with the easy ones.

(known as 'acclimatising') before joint preparation, as changes in moisture content are likely to cause movement, which will stress joints. Large stock can be broken down to close to final size before acclimatising, which both speeds up the process and makes storage simpler.

### What to Look For or Avoid

Knots and other defects should be avoided both within and close to joints as they challenge accurate preparation and weaken the finished joint. Straight, parallel grain will always work best, with quarter-sawn wood being more stable over time. Drawers are well known for displaying dovetails, and quarter-sawn wood is recommended to reduce the seasonal tightening or slackening in operation.

In order to more easily plane joints flush after assembly, give thought to the best planing direction when selecting individual boards and arranging them in a workpiece, and avoid overly figured or alternating grain.

Continuous grain match, where the wood grain appears to run uninterrupted – around a box, for example – is often a desirable feature. Achieving it requires material that starts out thick enough to yield two boards when sawn through its thickness, re-sawn. Bear in mind that the saw cut will waste some material, and in reality most re-sawn boards will move a little, bowing or twisting out of flat. After re-sawing, flattening and smoothing, a fair amount of the initial thickness can be lost, so extra thickness is allowed for. The continuous grain match process will be explained in Chapter 7.

### MOISTURE CONTENT

The following is a succinct description of moisture content given to me by Gervais Sawyer, a friend and wood expert:

> One of the problems with wood is that it is hygroscopic – that is to say, it gains or loses moisture according to the humidity of the surroundings.
>
> When wood is saturated or green it is much easier to work, but as it dries it will shrink. Taking a range from green to heated indoors, this shrinkage can be as much as 8 per cent. Because shrinkage can be different in different axes, shrinkage can cause distortion. Some timbers are better than others in this respect.
>
> With natural air drying, wood can dry down to 16 per cent or so, but in centrally heated environments can dry further, to 12 per cent. Air drying is cheap but uncontrollable. A few hot weeks in summer can cause huge damage in wood drying yards because the outside of boards dry rapidly around a wet core, causing built-in stresses that result in distortion or splits.
>
> A better solution, although at a cost, is to artificially (kiln) dry wood under controlled conditions. At the end of a drying cycle the wood is conditioned to remove any inherent stresses and should remain stable. Dry wood is denser and therefore more difficult to work than when green.

## TOOLS

With sufficient time and care you could cut many dovetail joints with just a sharp pocket knife – and that's not a bad challenge to try. Realistically though, just a few tools will make up a very capable, basic dovetailing kit. As the design and complexity of the joints you make increase, then you are likely to add to this kit in order to prepare them, or to prepare them more easily. Let's look at a basic kit of tools, and then consider how its contents might expand over time.

### Basic Kit

The following tools are recommended as a starting point, and are sufficient to begin your journey into dovetailing.

In addition to these tools, a means of holding workpieces while cutting is required, ideally a workbench with a vise, a bench hook, and some F-clamps.

When buying tools you could probably spend fifty times the cost of this book on just the basic kit, or you could spend far less than a tenth of that. Be assured, spending ten times as much for hand tools will not result in ten times better, or faster, dovetails. It is true that usually the more you spend, the better a tool will perform, but the cost rises exponentially compared to the performance improvement. Three important factors should be considered:

- Are the cutting tools sharp, or capable of being sharpened? Some tools will be razor sharp out of the box, others will need some degree of sharpening. Do you know how to sharpen, and do you have the resources to do it?
- Are the marking-out tools accurate? If your try-square isn't exactly 90 degrees, then you won't be able to lay out the dovetail pins or tails accurately.
- Are the tools comfortable to use as intended? An uncomfortable tool will be a constant distraction from the job in hand, and will lead to poor work.

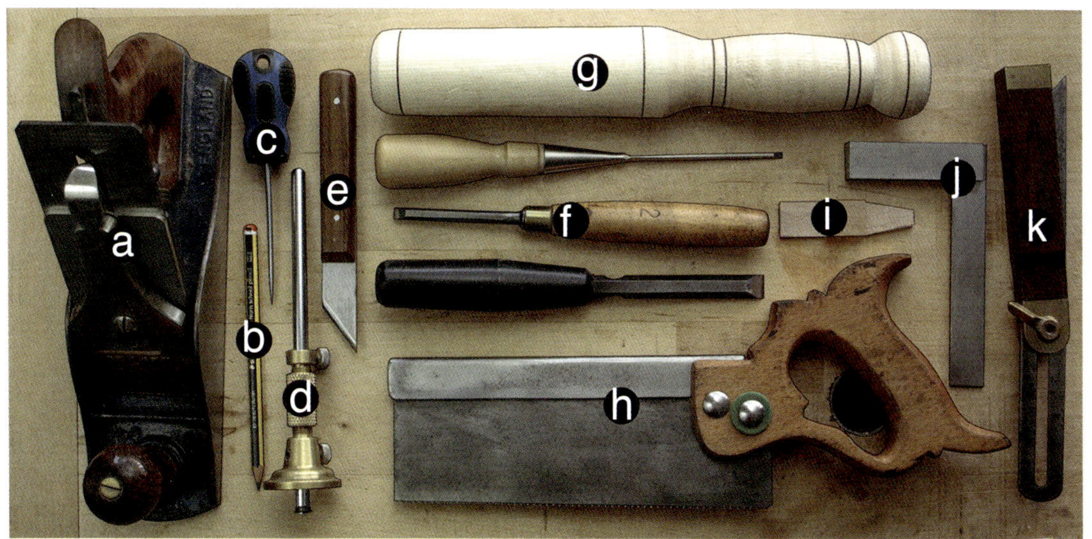


A basic kit of tools which, together with a workbench and work holding aids, will suffice for many dovetail varieties. a) Plane; b) Pencil; c) Awl; d) Marking gauge; e) Marking knife; f) Chisels; g) Mallet; h) Dovetail saw; i) Dovetail marking gauge; j) Try-square, k) Sliding bevel gauge.

| **Basic Tools Recommended for Dovetailing** | |
|---|---|
| Bench plane | To square the material prior to marking out, and to flush the joint surfaces once complete. A plane that is between a half and two times the length of the parts being joined is comfortable, so the equivalent of a Stanley no. 4 to no. 5½ would be suitable for most boxes and household furniture. |
| Pencil | To mark the lines defining the slope of tails or pins, and which areas are waste before its removal. |
| Awl | To transfer layout from pins to tails. A slim scalpel is usually fine as an alternative. |
| Marking gauge | To set and check consistent thickness in material prior to marking out, and to mark out the shoulders and baselines for the joints. |
| Marking knife | For defining shoulders and transferring layout from tails to pins. If pins are kept very slim, a thin scalpel is often required as well. |
| Bevel-edge chisels | To chop and pare waste. A range of sizes is definitely useful, but 3mm, 6mm and 12mm are a good start. |
| Mallet | A mallet is recommended over a hammer when chopping with a chisel, to avoid damage to chisel handles. |
| Back saw | A saw with a rigid back helps ensure the straight cuts needed for joints. A Western or Japanese dovetail saw, tenon saw or dozuki saw are all suitable. |
| Dovetail gauge | Ensures that the slope of tails or pins is consistent when marking out. A bevel gauge is a suitable alternative.<br> 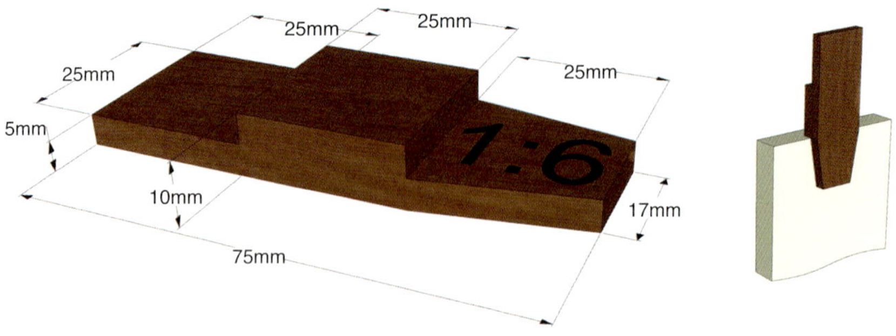<br>Design for a simple dovetail gauge made with just a few saw cuts. Make a few, with different slope angles as and when you need them. |
| Try-square | To check the squareness of material prior to marking out, and for squaring off the ends of tails and the sides of pins when marking out. I favour a small engineer's try-square for remaining square over time, but a small carpenter's try-square or accurate combination square will do. |
| Bevel gauge | Set to the correct angle for the tails, the gauge ensures that the slope of tails or pins is consistent when marking out. A dovetail gauge is an alternative, and can be shop made. |

A bench hook helps to hold a workpiece when sawing at a workbench. It is as simple as a short wide board with battens attached on each side at opposite ends.

F-clamps can hold a workpiece down to the bench, preventing it from moving around while chopping, and in the absence of a vice they can hold a workpiece vertically to the front of the bench for sawing or paring.

If you're not confident in selecting the right tools, ask for guidance from your local woodworking group, joiner, cabinet maker or trusted independent retailer, and try out the tool before buying, or buy on the understanding that you can return any tool that doesn't suit you.

### A SOLID WORKBENCH

A prerequisite for good joinery is a solid workbench. It is the basis for holding a workpiece steady and at the right height for layout and cutting operations. It can be purchased or home-made, and should be considered a valuable investment for a woodworker. Small, collapsible workbenches are not ideal, as their light weight will struggle to hold a workpiece steady during sawing, chopping or planing. However, in the absence of a solid workbench, they can be used together with a less vigorous cutting approach.

## Adding to the Basic Kit

Once you have started using basic dovetail joints in your projects, and you decide to continue and extend your range, you will find that the tools described in the table are desirable.

## Shop-Made Jigs

Jigs that are simple to make, such as a shooting board and the accessories for it, extend the dovetailing kit still further.

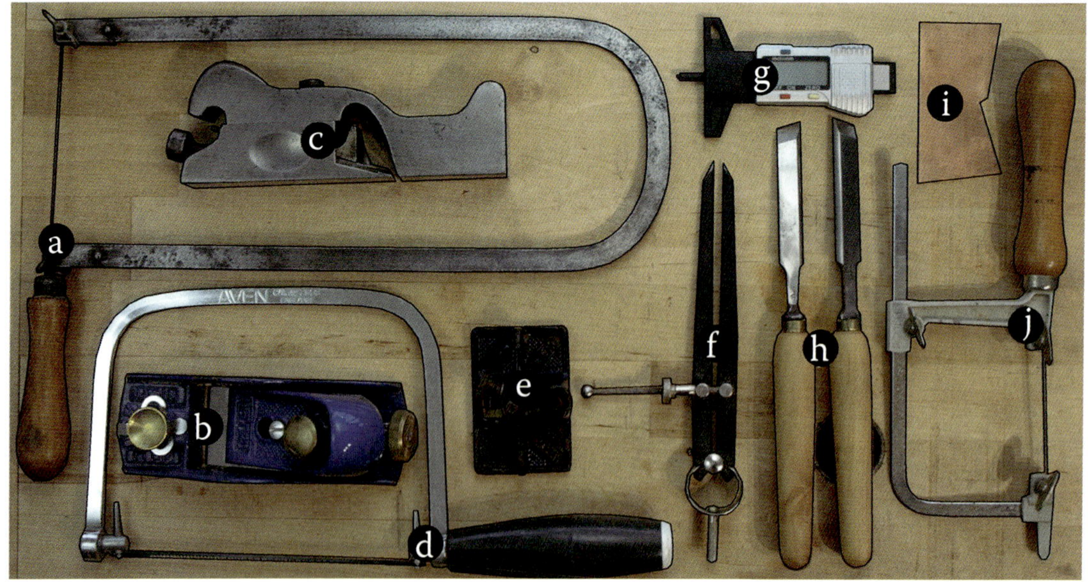


As you progress, your dovetailing tool kit will grow. Additional tools will increase ease and efficiency, and open up possibilities for complexity. a) Fretsaw; b) Low-angle block plane; c) Shoulder plane; d) Coping saw; e) Small router plane; f) Spring dividers; g) Depth gauge; h) Skew chisels (shop made); i) Flat dovetail template; j) Jeweller's saw.

| **Adding to the Basic Kit: More Useful Tools** | |
|---|---|
| Jeweller's saws, fretsaws or coping saws | Sawing bulk waste away between pins and tails, saves on chopping, which can reduce preparation time and be less risky in brittle or spongy wood. Jeweller's saws and fretsaws have slim blades, ideal for fine work. Standard coping-saw blades are more suited to rougher work in joinery. |
| Block plane (low-angle) | This tool quickly trims excess end grain from tails or pins, prior to using a smoothing bench plane. It is more suitable than a bench plane for smoothing small work. |
| Shoulder plane | Can be used to prepare mitres along a secret mitre dovetail or a mitred double-lap dovetail. |
| Router plane (small) | Cuts sockets to a consistent depth with little thought, and is most useful in larger work. Some wheel-style marking gauges can perform the same function, as can simple shop-made devices.<br><br>A passable mini-router can be made using a countersunk machine screw, a nut, and a piece of steel bar stock, drilled and tapped for the screw. The nut is used to lock the shaped cutter at the desired depth. My example has a rosewood shoe attached and a throat opening cut out. |
| Spring dividers | Useful for marking out evenly spaced tails or pins, and for repeating on multiple joints. |
| Depth gauge | An easy way to check that waste has been removed to the right depth. Alternatively a small router plane can be used. |
| Skew chisels | These chisels ease access to socket corners in lapped and secret dovetails. Essential only to maximise joint strength, since internal tail corners can be used instead. These can be shop-made by grinding standard bevel-edge chisels. |
| Flat dovetail template | Desirable for marking out lapped and double-lap dovetails with foreshortened pins, and also secret mitre dovetails.<br><br>Dimensions for a simple shop-made dovetail template. This can easily be cut from copper or zinc plate, and is used where three-dimensional dovetail marking gauges cannot reach. |

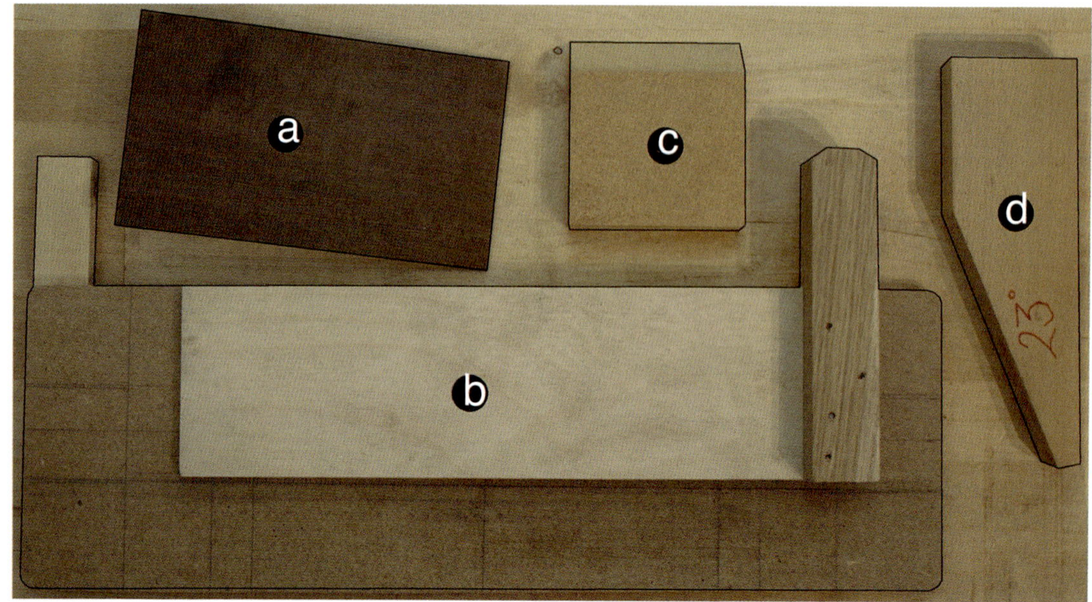


Extending the basic dovetail tool kit with shop-made jigs that help prepare the ends of workpieces accurately, ready for jointing. a) Horizontal ramp; b) Shooting board; c) Mitre guide block; d) Vertical ramp.

| **Simple-to-Make Jigs** | |
|---|---|
| Mitre guide block | Guides a shoulder plane or paring chisel when cutting secret mitre dovetail or mitred double-lap dovetail mitres. These are made as required by cross-cutting a board at half of the required joint angle (for example 45 degrees for a right-angle joint) and planing it true using a mitre square or bevel gauge to check. |
| Shooting board and ramps | As well as trimming board ends to 90 degrees, with the addition of ramps it becomes an almost essential tool for the preparation of boards for bevelled and double-bevel dovetails. Not too different to a bench hook, a shooting board usually has a sub-base on which a bench plane slides on its side, and its fence extends to the edge of the main base. Ramps can be either solid or made up with sheet material glued to different sized spacers. |
| Dovetail alignment jig | Large square corner joint with fences attached, to which a tailboard and pin-board can be clamped in alignment when transferring layout. If you struggle with the methods for alignment that I recommend, then give this a go. |
| Twin-screw vise | Holds wide boards flat and raises the work to a comfortable height for joint preparation. These can be made from thick boards coupled together with commercial or shop-made hardware or clamps. |

A mitre guide block clamped to a secret mitre dovetail pin board gives a reference surface for a paring chisel or shoulder plane to travel on, removing the chance of freehand inaccuracies.

A shop-made, bench-mounted twin-screw vise (or Moxon vise) raises work closer to your eyeline, whilst holding it secure. Wide boards can be accommodated, ideal for dovetail joints in bigger projects.

A shooting board, not much more than a bench hook in construction, helps the accurate truing of square ends of boards, when used with a bench plane on its side. The dimensions given are a guide.

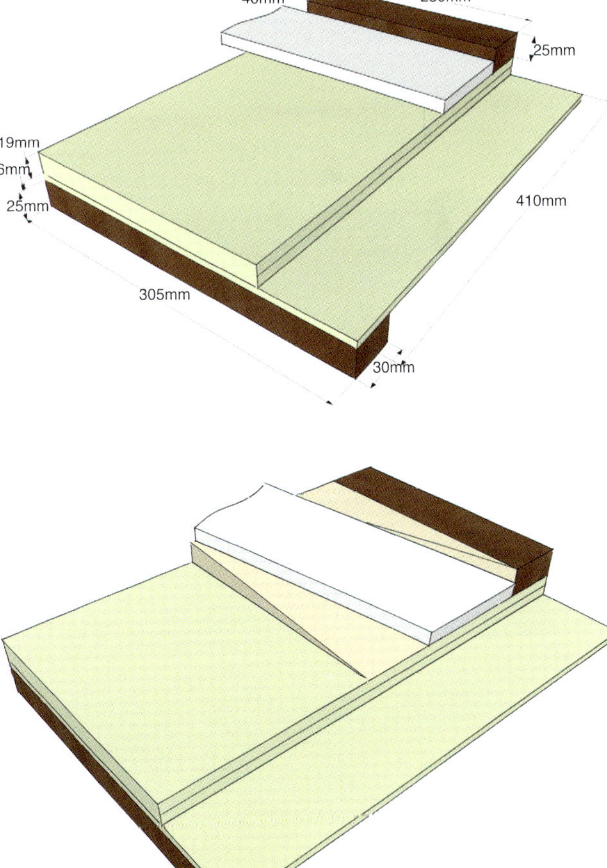


Adding horizontal and vertical ramps to a shooting board allows angled and compound-angled ends on boards to be shot with a plane.

CHAPTER 2

# TECHNIQUES

This chapter introduces woodworking techniques – tips or tricks if you like – that could easily fill a book by themselves. I'll cover those that should help in your dovetail joinery. Those techniques that I feel will help most in terms of accuracy, appearance and speed, plus some alternatives to the standard dovetailing techniques, are given in further chapters.

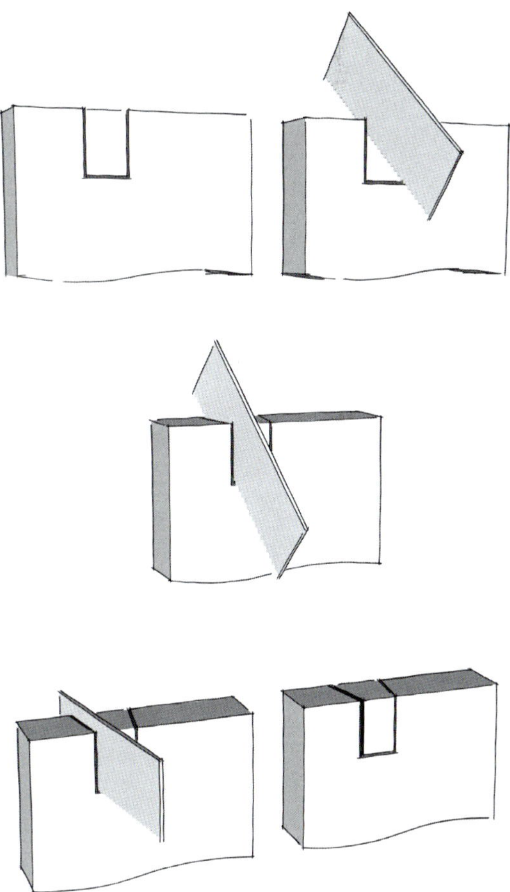

## SAWING TRUE AND PLUMB

Joints that need to slide together, such as the dovetail joints in this book, require well mating surfaces. In the case of dovetail joints, and others, these mating surfaces are flat, and are produced primarily by sawing with a rigid blade. Apart from the initial stage of a cut, the rigid blade helps to guide the saw on a straight path. With this in mind, it is crucial to start cuts correctly. Until this becomes second nature to you, follow the two-line and three-line methods, and practise making sets of parallel plumb cuts each time you go to the workshop.

### The Two-Line Method

The two-line method is quickest, requiring only two marking-out lines to saw up against, and

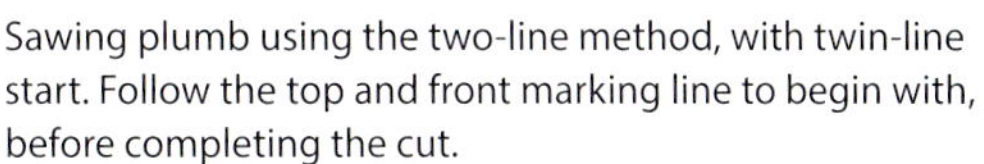

Sawing plumb using the two-line method, with twin-line start. Follow the top and front marking line to begin with, before completing the cut.

Stanley No. 71 router plane in action. A router plane is not essential for hand-cut dovetails, but is certainly desirable. Small router planes are especially useful for smaller corner joints in cabinet making.

relying on this initial sawing to maintain the plane in which the saw continues to complete the cut. This is also the method where any lap is required, with the remaining cut being made with chisels.

The saw cut can be advanced along either one or both of the lines to start with. If both, then the cut proceeds until the teeth reach the ends, whereupon the third side is cut by sawing whilst pivoting the toothline at the bottom of the first line.

If you find that watching both lines at the same time is too difficult, it is possible to start the saw cutting against just one marking line, across the top, only to half bury the teeth – this sets the toothline in one direction, then saw down against the second line whilst pivoting the toothline at the far end. From there, the cut is completed as before.

### Three-Line Method

For through dovetails, a three-line method, although slower, is advisable when cutting large joints in thick boards, where a small deviation of saw-plate angle can show up as a significant error on the reverse side of the board.

Proceed as the two-line method, but to cut the third side, reverse the work and follow the third mark-out line, pivoting the toothline in the top cut. This leaves an internal triangle to saw through, guided by the kerfs on each side.

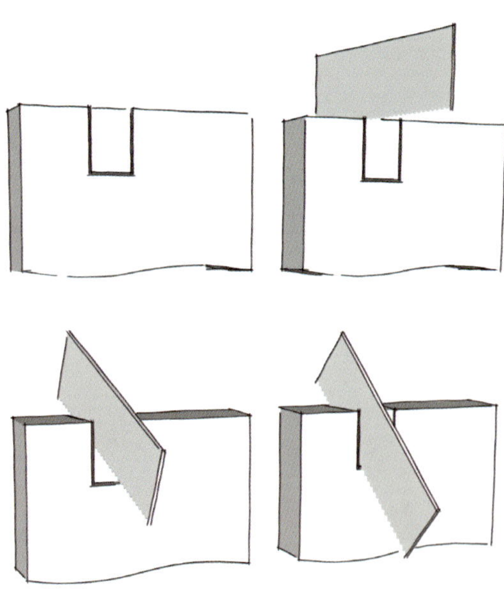

Starting the two-line method for sawing plumb by first sawing a kerf to half the tooth height. Then concentrate on following the vertical line.

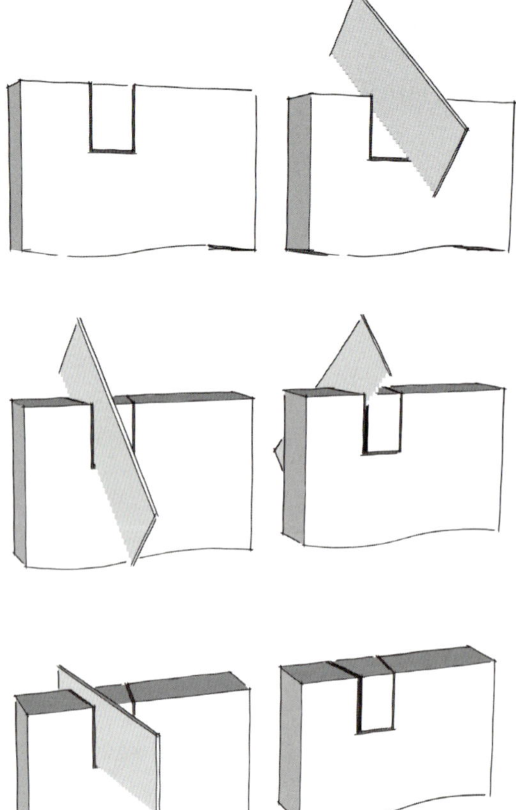

For sawing thicker boards, the three-line method can be used to help assure plumb cuts on both faces of the board.

## TIPS FOR SAWING TAILS AND PINS

Always try to cut into the show surface of tail- and pinboards, so that you can see where to stop, and so that any fibre tearout is on the reverse side.

### Tails

- Tilt the tailboard in the vise at the same slope as the dovetails, so that you can saw plumb to the workbench: this should be easier than sawing with the saw tilted over. Don't forget to reposition the board when sawing the other side of the tails.
- Gang multiple tailboards together, and cut as one. The extra width helps to keep the cuts square.

### Pins

- Clamp a bevel gauge to the pinboard, set to the angle you are cutting. This gives you a much longer reference against which to align the saw plate.
- Stand at an angle to the bench so that your shoulder, elbow, wrist and the saw all line up with the direction you need to cut.

## CHOPPING AND PARING

The importance of sharp tools is a prerequisite to good joint preparation, but even the sharpest edge can produce unwanted effects. In dovetail joinery we are mostly concerned with the use of chisels to remove waste and leave flat joint surfaces, but we must be aware of their tendency to both grip material and act as a wedge.

### Wedge Effect of a Chisel

Since a standard chisel bevel is on just one side of the blade, as the chisel is driven into the wood, the wedge effect exerts a force on the chisel towards the non-bevel side or back. The chisel is pushed out of line with where it started, as can be seen above. All the care taken to knife the shoulder (or baseline) of the joint can easily be wiped out.

To minimise the wedge effect, material on the bevel side of the chisel should be cleared as much as possible. There are two main ways to achieve this: either by sawing the waste away close to the shoulder line with a fretsaw or

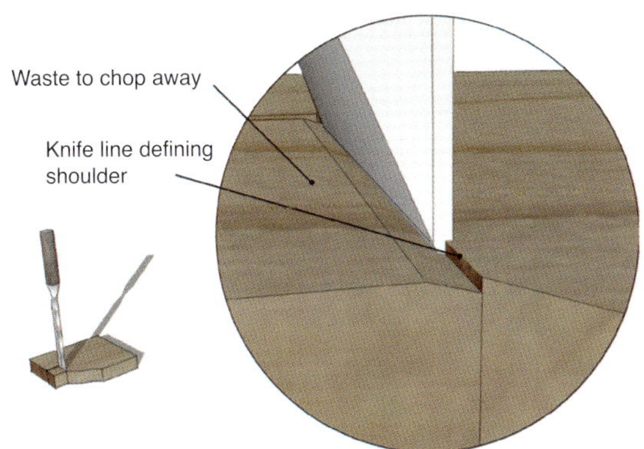


When chopping waste with a chisel, the bevel acts as a wedge and moves the back of the chisel through the knifed shoulder line.

Clockwise from top left: to preserve a knife line, first make a shallow chop offset slightly from the line, then notch out to the depth of the chop and chop again. Repeat until close to full depth, before chopping directly on the line.

similar, or by notching out the waste, bit by bit, initially staying shy of the shoulder line.

### Chip Grab

'Chip grab' is the term I use to describe the plucking out of end-grain material by a chisel. Most notably this appears to happen on softer woods, especially wood softened by spalting or other causes. This soft wood seems to grab the sharp edge, resisting a push cut, and a chip is pulled from the end grain.

Chip grab should be predicted and then avoided by sawing as much waste as possible, carefully, and then paring with gentle shearing cuts using a freshly honed chisel with a low bevel angle.

Material can be pulled from the end grain when chopping pin or tail waste, in what I call 'chip grab'. Learn how to predict it, so that you can take avoiding action.

A sharp chisel with a low bevel angle and a side-to-side action is usually sufficient to avoid chip grab in tight spots between pins or tails.

Prediction comes from previous experience of a wood species, and testing offcuts from as close as possible to the area to be cut. Shearing cuts in tight spaces, such as between tails or pins, can be achieved by side-to-side sweeps of the chisel tip.

## PARING TO LINES

Precise joinery uses knife lines for marking out. A single bevel knife, held perpendicular to the surface, leaves a sharp, perpendicular, and well defined line for registration of a chisel edge. Saw cuts can be made just shy of these lines, removing the majority of the waste, before final paring cuts are made with a chisel, using the knife line as a reference for the chisel back. An example of the process of paring to the lines is shown below.

The example shows a case where paring cuts can be made from three different directions, but a similar approach can be taken in other situations.

The steps recommended when paring waste from a knifed corner for precise joinery. *Top left*: Upwards from the knife line, from two opposite sides. *Top right:* A third cut is made from the adjacent side to the first two, leaving an angled hump of waste with a clear knife shelf around its perimeter. *Bottom right:* Thin paring cuts are now made parallel to the knife shelf, without risk of removing the knife lines. *Bottom left:* Final waste is removed while keeping the chisel edges flat on the knife lines and shy of the board edges, to leave a perfect flat plane.

## EXCAVATING CORNERS

To prepare wholly precise dovetails it is necessary to remove waste right up into some acute corners. There is a workaround for where these corners do not meet a show surface, but first let us look at the basic problems and the appropriate solutions.

### Through Dovetails

A regular bevel-edge chisel can cut into the corner between a tail side and the shoulder of a through-dovetail tailboard, but its small square section below the bevels will restrict its access when cutting between tails if used square to the tailboard.

By taking a narrower chisel and skewing the cut, the tip of the chisel can reach right into the base of the tail unencumbered, and the waste can be pared away cleanly.

### Lapped Dovetails

In lapped dovetails of any kind, pinboards have acute corners between three surfaces – the bottom, back and side of the sockets. The sides of the sockets, the pin surface, can be accessed with a normal bevel-edge chisel, but the bottom and back of the socket cannot be cleaned right into the corner.

To cut right into this acute corner, a slim, pointed knife blade can be used, although a pair of dedicated skew chisels are easier to use and produce a clean cut. The skew of the chisel tip prevents the non-cutting corner of the blade from fouling the back of the socket when paring the bottom, and vice versa. A pair of skew chisels are required to reach both left and right corners.

A simple solution for paring the internal corners is to skew the chisel a little. To do this, the chisel must be considerably narrower than the gap between the tails.

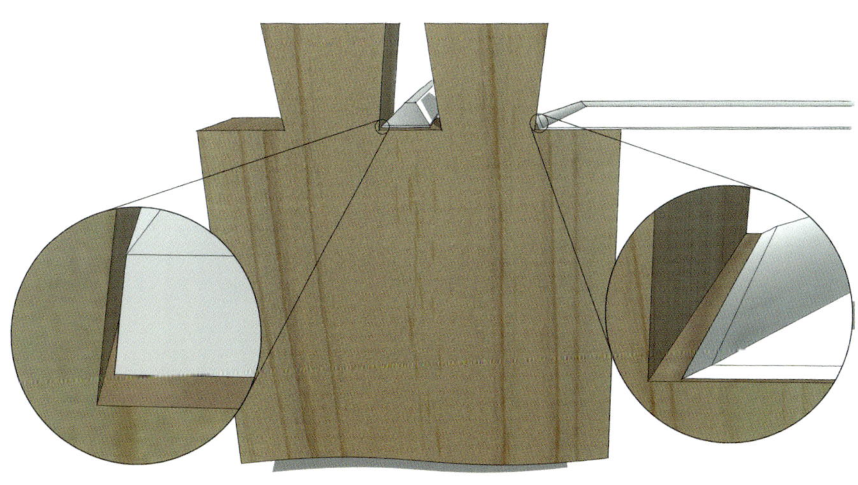

There is a potential access problem when paring square between tails, due to the shape of the chisel. However, accessing the outside corner of the extreme tails presents no such challenge.

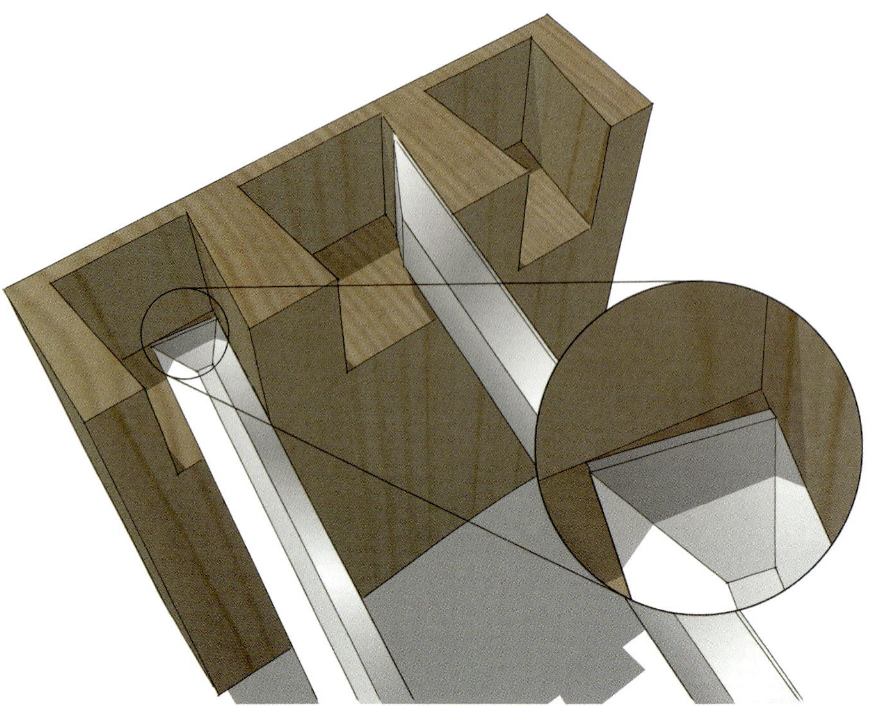

A square-ended chisel cannot cut into an acute corner because of the geometry.

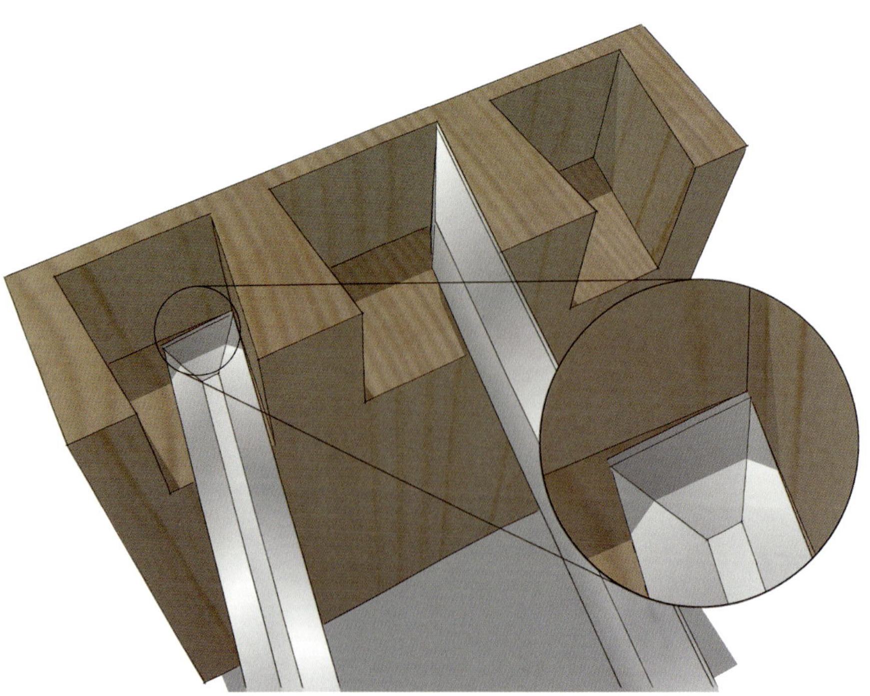

Using a skew chisel allows access to the acute corner in a lapped pinboard. The chisels extending corner tip can pare between the bottom and side, in this case, right into the back wall.

## SPACING TAILS AND PINS

In joints with multiple tails there are three options for sizing and spacing them out: random, equal, or custom.

### Random Sizing and Spacing

Random sizing and spacing is the quickest to mark out, but usually results in a poor appearance, and can also end up confounding a woodworker where the waste required to be removed is narrower than their smallest chisel.

Consider using this spacing for non-show surfaces, such as the rear joints of drawers, where you might even forgo the marking out of the initial tails, or pins, and simply saw them from experience. The speed benefit of the latter is clear, but it is not for the novice.

I shall concentrate mainly on equally sized and spaced layouts, as well as custom layouts: in both cases thought should be given to the size of the waste areas so that access is sufficient for the chisels available.

### Equal Sizing and Spacing

Equal sizing and spacing is my term for where all the pins and half-pins are identical in width, and all the tails are identical to each other. This can sometimes look machine cut at first glance, especially where the tail width is identical to the pin width, but it is easy to mark out, as shown in the illustration.

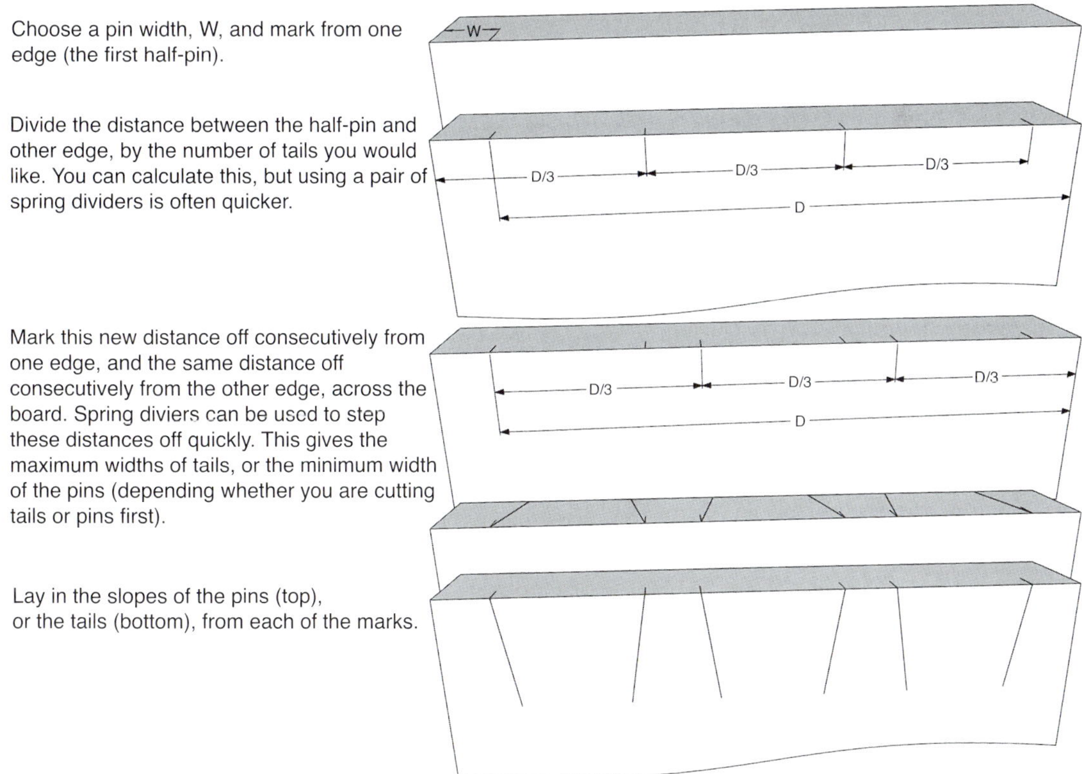


Marking out for three equally sized and spaced dovetails, with equal width pins. A pair of spring dividers can be used both to determine the fractional distance, and to prick all the necessary points along the edge.

## Equal Tails and Equal Pins

Where all the tails are identical in width, and all the whole pins are identical in width, I term equal tails and equal pins. In this case the half-pins do not need to be the same width as each other. This looks a little less machine cut than equal sizing and spacing, and is still fairly easy to mark out, as shown in the illustration.

## Custom Sizing and Spacing

My preference for appearance is what I term custom sizing and spacing, and it strongly suggests that a joint is both bespoke and hand cut. Marking out is generally more time consuming, and multiple pairs of spring dividers are a definite advantage.

One way of making the layout look designed rather than random is to randomly lay out one half of the joint, and then mirror the layout on the other half. The symmetry of this approach is the key. An alternative is to repeat a layout section again and again.

Custom spacing of dovetails can produce many forms, some more appealing than others. Depending on the complexity, marking out can be tedious and these joints should only be used where they will be seen.

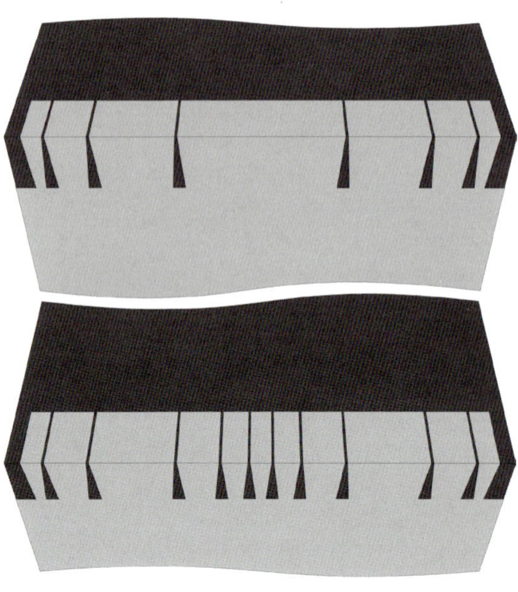

Two examples of custom sizing and spacing dovetails where symmetry maintains a certain order. Repeating patterns can likewise achieve the same result.

Choose half-pin widths, and mark from appropriate edges.

hp1

hp2

Divide the distance between half-pins plus any gap required between tails, by the number of tails required. Mark this new distance off consecutively from both half-pins, across the board, preferably using spring dividers.

hp1

hp2

(D+d)/3

(D+d)/3

(D+d)/3

(D+d)/3

D

d = desired gap

Lay in the slopes of the pins, or the tails, from each of the marks.

Where the width of end pins differs, either from each other or from the intermediate pins, a slightly different method is used for marking out from where they are all equal.

## USING A BEVEL GAUGE TO LAY OUT DOVETAILS

Although dovetail markers are easily available in the common slope ratios, such as 1:5, 1:7, it is definitely worth knowing how to set a bevel gauge to these, and any other ratio. Marking out for bevelled dovetails will be greatly aided, and the long blade of a bevel gauge will allow the largest of dovetails to be marked easily.

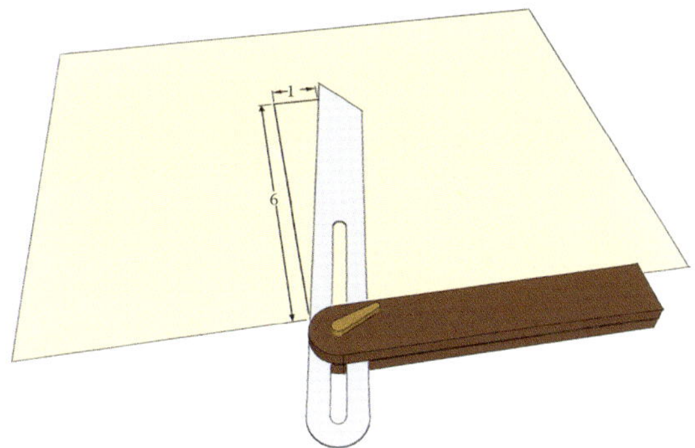


Setting a bevel gauge to a slope of 1:6 using lines drawn perpendicular and parallel to a straight edge of a board.

### How to Set a Bevel Gauge

Let us use, for example, a slope of 1:6. Take a flat board with a straight edge (you could even use the top of the workbench), and use a try-square and ruler to draw a perpendicular line from the edge to a point 6cm (2.4in) away. Draw a line from this point, parallel to the edge of the board, a distance of 1cm (0.4in). Set the stock of the gauge against the edge of the board and line up the blade to close a triangle with the two drawn lines. Lock the gauge with the lever, or screw, and it is now ready to use on the tailboard or pinboard.

## GANG-CUTTING TAILS

When preparing the tails of dovetails first, and where multiple tailboards require the same layout, the tailboards can be ganged together for marking out and sawing. Sawing them together like this is a little quicker, but the main advantage is the width of the cut, which helps keep the saw aligned square to the boards. As we will see later, squareness will help prevent joints from tightening excessively during assembly, or showing gaps on the outside once assembled.

Gang-cutting tails is quicker, and potentially more accurate as the square line being cut to is substantially longer.

## BEVELLING TAILS

Adding bevels to tails can help two common problems in dovetail preparation.

### Assembling Well Fitting Joints

Where joints have been prepared to a very close fit, which is the ideal goal, assembling them, especially once glue is applied, can be tricky, as any slight misalignment will prevent the tails sliding between the pins. By adding a small bevel to the entry sides of the tails, the parts help to align themselves, and in addition protect the crisp pin edges from being damaged.

### Difficult to Clear Waste in Acute Corners

Waste in the bottom rear corners of lapped joints will prevent the tails from seating correctly in the sockets. Removing a corresponding amount of material from the tails by bevelling the hidden tail corners leaves room for the waste, and allows the joint to close properly.

## TRANSFERRING LAYOUT

Where possible, layout is transferred from the first cut part to the second part, rather than trying to lay out both parts from planned measurements. The advantage is that any deviations when cutting the first part can be corrected.

### Cutting the Pins First

Where pins are cut first, access for tracing the layout of the pins to the tailboard can be restricted. An awl, a pointed scalpel or an engineering pencil are reasonable choices when this is the case.

A pointed scalpel blade can often be the solution where access to transfer-pin layout to a tailboard is restricted (*top*), especially in smaller work, and when there is little space between tails to transfer their layout to a pinboard (*bottom*).

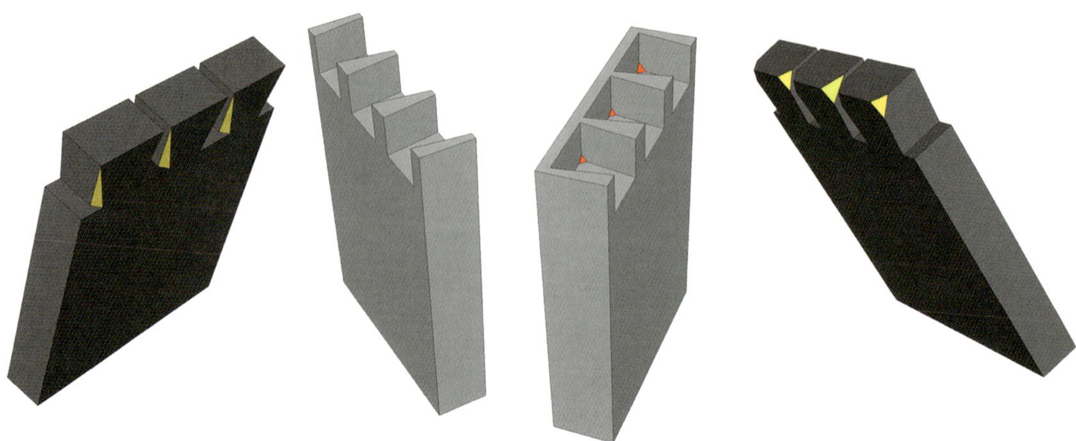

Adding bevels to tails can help parts to align and to seat properly during assembly, where the fit is good and/or waste material is not completely removed from sockets.

## Cutting the Tails First

Where tails are cut first, so long as they are not lapped, access is usually easier and traditional marking knives and pencils should present no problems. Where very fine pins are desired, the tail-to-tail gap is minimal, and a much thinner blade, such as a scalpel, will need to be used.

To increase contrast on end grain when using a knife to transfer layout, electrical or masking tape can be applied to the joint area. Once the layout has been knifed, the tape covering the waste areas is removed, leaving a clear line to saw to.

## Salt or Sugar for Friction

To help prevent parts from moving while transferring layout I recommend adding a few granules of table salt between them. When pressed together the granules dig in and prevent the parts sliding or rotating. This is also an excellent tip for when gluing parts together that have no inherent means to stay in position.

## Steel Rule or Rebate Alignment

Aligning the tailboard and pinboard when transferring the joint layout can sometimes elude beginners, and the use of a steel rule or rebate can help. The principle is that a positive register is created at the baseline of the tailboard against which the pinboard can be aligned.

The steel rule technique shown in the illustration involves clamping a steel rule across the tailboard, aligned with the baseline. The pinboard can then be positioned against the edge of the ruler.

Tape can be useful to highlight the pinboard layout where knife lines in the end grain are difficult to see. The tape is cut through during the transfer stage, and sections peeled away to reveal the waste areas.

## TIPS FOR MARKING OUT IMPLEMENTS

### Pencils

- Sharpen pencils regularly, as a blunt tip will mark away from the pin or tail, indicating the wrong place to saw.
- Retractable pencils often have a collar that can offset a barely exposed lead from where it should be marking.
- White pencils offer great contrast when marking dark woods, and are especially clear for hatching in areas of waste material.

### Pens

- Fine-tip pens avoid the need for sharpening, but check that the marked line is tight to the pins or tails that are being transferred.
- Select pens that dry fast and don't wick into the wood grain.

### Awl

- A long bevel to the tip will prevent an awl's knee from throwing the point out.
- Dedicate a dovetailing awl, and bend the tip over for easier access.
- Machinists' combined straight and bent-tip scribes are a wonderful alternative to a woodworkers' awl.

### Knife

- For double-bevel knives, tilt the knife and rest a bevel against the pin or tail, so the blade edge is tight to the corner.
- Left- and right-handed single-bevel knives can be used with the bevel away from the pin or tail.
- Be careful not to cut the pins or tails of the template part as you draw the knife around them.

The rebate technique involves planing a rebate across the inside of the tailboard from the end to the baseline, leaving a little shoulder for registering the pinboard against.

Personally I find it easier to align the boards directly by sight, with the method I use in the preparation chapters.

## Saw Transfer Alternate Kerf Offset

This is also known as the credit-card method. I came up with this method of marking out in an attempt to speed up the preparation of randomly spaced finger (box) joints, only to find equivalent examples online. I include it here as an alternative method for transferring pinboard layout from a tailboard, where it also works very well.

The standard way to transfer the layout from a tailboard to a pinboard is to complete the tailboard preparation, then knife round the tails while the tailboard is held in place against the pinboard end grain. With experience this is a quick and accurate method, and it is how the joints described in this book will be shown.

By comparison, the credit-card method is a little slower, but doesn't depend on accurate knife use, and gives clear and positive registration for saw placement.

**The Theory**

The theory behind the credit-card method is that the area of material to be removed from the pinboard is equivalent to that left on the tailboard, and that the initial saw cuts should be made within that area. By offsetting the tailboard, first to one side, by the thickness of a saw kerf, one edge of each tail will now provide an accurate guide to start sawing, whilst offsetting it to the other side will align the other edge of each tail to the correct position for guiding the saw.

Using a spacer to offset the tailboard from the pinboard, first to the left, then to the right, by a single saw kerf, allows the heel of the saw to start the cut in the correct position.

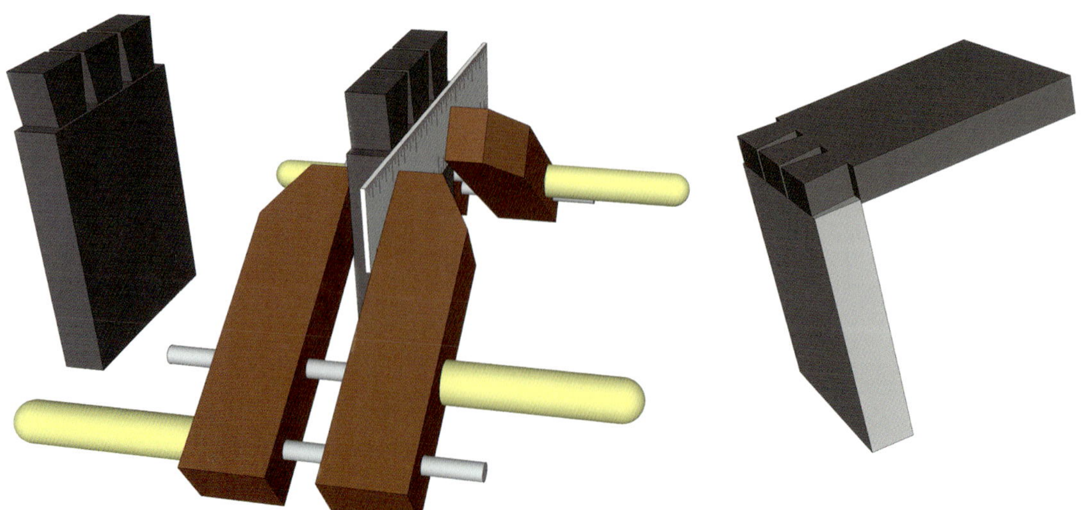

A rebate behind the tails on a tailboard, or a steel rule clamped on to it, provides a solid reference for the pinboard during layout transfer.

**The Method**

In practice, a spacer the thickness of a saw kerf is used to offset the tailboard the correct distance, and then the heel of the saw is used to begin a cut. The heel of the saw is used with a pull cut, thus saving the toe from crashing into the baseline of the tailboard (for pull saws, such as a Japanese dovetail saw or dozuki, the toe would be used rather than the heel).

By transferring the layout immediately after making the sloped tail cuts, the heel of the saw is held in the saw kerfs, reducing any chance of it moving out of alignment. Offset the tailboard to the right to start the saw cuts on the left of the tails, then offset it to the left to start the saw cuts on the right of the tails. A couple of pull cuts with a sharp dovetail saw will establish a saw kerf in the pinboard, which can then be extended to the baseline of the pins.

Offset the tailboard to the left, to mark all the right-hand sides of the tails, before offsetting it to the right and marking all the left-hand sides.

**Credit Card**

When I first experimented with this method, I made an end-grain cut with my dovetail saw and looked for something that was a sliding fit in the kerf. It needed to be flat and have a consistent thickness, and a credit card was ideal.

Different saws will have different sized kerfs, so if you try this method you may require a different thickness of spacer. Perhaps a piece of veneer, a steel rule or a card scraper will suit.

## FIXING GAPS

Sometimes the prepared joint will display gaps when the tail- and pinboards are assembled. When practising, these can be left as a record of progress, but when the joint is to be part of a project then it should be fixed or replaced.

With modern adhesives, the occasional gap between a tail side and its corresponding pin side can often be ignored with respect to joint

For this dovetail saw, a club card or credit card is a perfect fit in the kerf, and will offset the boards the right amount. For your own saw you may need to find an alternative spacer.

Gaps, no matter their size, can spoil the appearance of a finished joint. Where they are not too numerous or excessive, or there is no option to prepare them again, there are ways to disguise them.

strength. However, there are two caveats: the joint should not be subject to abnormally high loads, and the outside tails should be a good fit to ensure that the edges remain tight.

Fixing alternatives fall into three categories, each with its own advantages and disadvantages.

## Prepare the Joint Again

Where there is enough length in the parts being prepared, cut away the first attempt and try again. Often the error occurs in transferring the layout and cutting the second part, whether starting with pins or tails, and in this case only the scribed part need be fixed. For example, if you cut the tails first and then cut some pins that were too narrow, cut off all the pins, re-scribe from the tails, and cut the pins more accurately.

## Build Up and Re-Cut

The next best solution, and ideal where there is no option to prepare the joint again, is to build up the pins where gaps occur, transfer the layout once more, and pare the sides of the pins to the lines.

Each gap is assessed, and the surface to be built up decided upon. The choice of building up the pins, rather than the tails, is usually taken because the majority of dovetail joints are lapped, and so only the end grain of the pins is visible, and the inserted material is less obvious. With through dovetails, the choice will depend on matching both face and end grain of either tails or pins, and there is no rule of thumb for that.

Offcuts of the original material are used to prepare well matched shims to glue on these surfaces. When dried, the shims are flushed to the boards and trimmed back until the joint can be assembled, leaving no gaps.

If the strength of an individual pin or tail is significantly compromised by having been cut too thin, then the shim can be scarfed further back into the board to provide extra strength.

## Filling

Filling is better than leaving gaps, and can sometimes prove to be almost invisible, but it adds little strength compared to properly

Dealing with gaps by building up the undersized pin and paring to the correct size and shape. Close-matching material leads to a near invisible fix.

building up, as clean and well fitted surfaces are needed for good glue adhesion.

Of the filling options, carefully selected and cut shims pressed into gaps with glue are preferable to mixing glue and sawdust to produce a stuffing compound, although this is a perfectly good option for small gaps.

Commercial fillers, although easy to use, rarely make for an invisible solution, unless carefully stained to match the base wood colour, and figure detail added to the surface.

## Peening

As woodworkers, the idea of deforming a part with a hammer might seem abhorrent, so what rôle does peening have? Perhaps the most annoying gaps are those that just show as a hairline. A cross-peen hammer, or some such alternative, is used to distort the pin and tail end grain such that the gap disappears.

Over time, and with alternating changes in moisture content, such distortions may revert, revealing the gaps again. In order to make a

Using glue mixed with fine sawdust to fill narrow gaps: a quick and easy way to disguise a poorly fitted joint line, at least from a distance.

Using a cross-peen hammer to close a gap between the tail and pin. Indentations are left from the blows, but these can be planed down to leave a smooth surface.

permanent fix, peening should be done during assembly while the joint is glued, such that the joint surfaces adhere to each other.

Leaving a little additional length in the tails and pins is advantageous, since peening will leave indentations that can then be planed away once the joint has cured.

Planing on to the joint surfaces will prevent breakout of splinters from the tails or pins, but may cause tearout in the face of boards, depending on their grain.

## FLUSHING JOINTS

No matter how good the joint preparation is, the glued joint is most unlikely to present as perfectly flush. Indeed, a little extra allowance is sensible if an exact finish size is required, as this can be crept up on with judicious planing.

A sudden step of just 0.025mm (1/1,000in) between the two parts of a joint will be detectable by touch, and will carry through many finishes. This is undesirable, and in the case of fine work must be corrected.

Sanding can certainly remove such a sudden step, but at the same time it can easily destroy the flatness of the surface. A more appropriate, and usually faster method of flushing joints, is to use a plane.

Excess pin or tail material can be quickly reduced with a block plane, planing from air towards the joint to avoid splintering or breakout.

Once the joint is close to flush, a fine-set smoothing plane will allow the joint to be planed fully flush; if sufficiently long, the smoothing plane will also help to keep the whole surface flat.

Attention should be paid to the best direction in which to plane the length of the pinboard and tailboard. If possible, select stock such that planing from air towards the joint doesn't cause tearout in the long grain. In many cases, the existence of adjacent joints in the boards will prevent such a simple approach. Wherever the grain direction is a concern, a couple of methods can help:

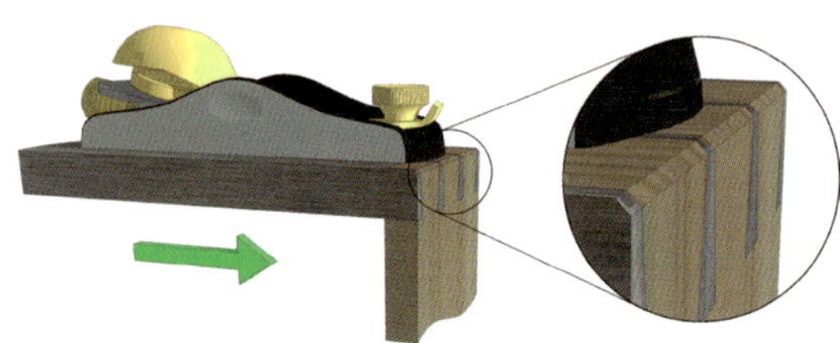

Planing flush into air using a small corner bevel to help prevent splinter breakout: a solution to contrary grain close to the joint, which can't be planed in the other direction without tearout.

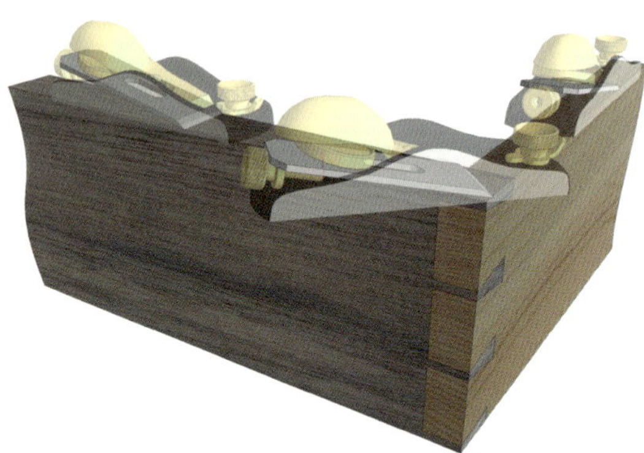

Planing the edges of a joint flush by turning the plane round the corner in a smooth motion, following the optimum planing direction for both boards.

- A scraper plane, or a back bevel on the bench plane iron, can be used to facilitate always planing from air towards the joint, at the expense of extra effort propelling the plane.
- Planing a small bevel across the corner of the joint will give support to the end grain whilst planing flush off the joint, or into air.

Planing the edges of joints should follow the grain direction too, where possible, turning the plane as the iron passes from one board to the other.

Where the grain directions do not oblige, stopped shavings can be taken, to or from the joint line, or the plane shifted towards the outside, where through shavings are possible, such that the iron only cuts the one board.

## SETTING A MARKING GAUGE

Much use will be made of marking gauges when doing dovetail work, and being able to set them accurately is important. I find the wheel style of marking gauge easiest to use, although I frequently use the more traditional wooden pin gauge or an adapted cutting gauge.

All these gauges can be set from a steel rule, the end of which is the zero point on the scale and is set against the gauge fence.

The shaft or beam of the gauge holding the wheel, pin or knife point is then advanced until the marking device reaches the desired distance on the rule. The gauge is then locked with the thumb screw, or wedge, and is ready to use.

More useful, I find, is to set the distance directly from the part which is being gauged for. For example, to gauge the thickness of a tailboard when dovetailing, the tailboard is substituted for the steel rule.

A big advantage of the wheel-style marking gauges, at least where the cutting edge of the wheel extends beyond the beam and any fitting screw, is that settings can be made by resting the fence on the part, and dropping the beam over the edge until the wheel contacts an underlying flat reference. This I find invaluable as my eyesight deteriorates with age.

Setting a marking gauge directly from the workpiece is more reliable than measuring the workpiece and then setting the gauge with a rule.

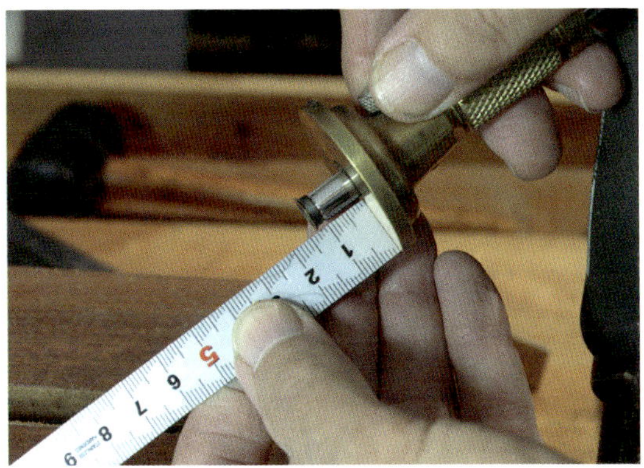

Setting a marking gauge to a specific measurement, by reference to a steel rule. The end of the rule should be undamaged to ensure an accurate setting.

Many wheel-style marking gauges can be set directly without relying on one's eyes.

CHAPTER 3

# FIRST JOINTS

The time to start dovetailing is almost here. We'll start with the basics and work gradually through to the more challenging joints. Expect to make some mistakes since all new skills are learned with practice. Most of all enjoy the experience: if you begin to get frustrated, take a break, re-read the instructions for the joint you are on, and if you're unsure then recap the earlier joints.

Dovetail joints are either 'in line' or 'cross grain.' It makes little difference, but we will cover both in the first two joints, the common dovetail and the dovetail halving. These two joints will introduce the basic practice needed to proceed to the joints that follow them, so take your time to learn and digest all the individual steps, which will be given in the greatest detail here, and less so as progress is made.

To round off the chapter I'll show the preparation of probably the two most iconic dovetail joints, the through dovetail and the lapped dovetail corner joints. Used extensively in drawer and carcass construction even today, albeit mostly machine cut, knowing how to cut these joints well can take your woodworking up a level.

## THE COMMON DOVETAIL

The common dovetail is by far the simplest corner dovetail joint, and is used extensively to give mechanical strength to framework, such as that surrounding trellis or lattice panels. It can also be found in furniture, and the framing of some timber buildings.

### Initial Stock Preparation

To greatly improve the ease and accuracy of marking out and the strength and appearance of the completed joint, the two parts should be carefully prepared. Traditional face side and face edge marking is recommended to help avoid

Possibly the simplest dovetail joint, the common dovetail is the starting point for all dovetail corner joints cut in line with the grain.

Some of the simple dovetail joints covered in this chapter.

alignment mistakes, although any system that clearly identifies the different sides and edges of the joining boards will suffice.

Knowing which end of each part is to be joined is also helpful, and I tend to use either a number or letter for each joint in a project, marking them on the corresponding ends of parts. Consistency is key, so both face sides should end up on the same side, and both face edges should end up on the same edge of the completed joint.

In preparing the stock, follow the guidelines below:

- All long grain faces should be flat.
- Where the finished parts are to be flush at the joint, they should be the same width.
- The thickness of parts can be different, but each part should have a consistent thickness (at least in the area of the joint).
- Parts should be squared all round.
- Ends should be prepared square to both the face side and face edge.

This initial preparation is the basis of most dovetail corner joints, and should become second nature. Of course there are some exceptions, which are pointed out in the box following.

### EXCEPTIONS TO STOCK PREPARATION GUIDELINES

There will be times when the basic stock preparation guidelines for dovetails won't do. For example, there are circumstances where parts will be of different widths, such as the back of a drawer that allows the base to slide beneath it, and in these cases the narrower part can be thought of as being joined to an equal-width section of the wider part.

In addition there are times where the parts will meet at an angle other than 90 degrees, and their ends should be prepared accordingly.

These and other cases will be covered as they occur later in the book.

## Marking Out and Cutting

There are two orders in which the joint can be marked out, known as pins first or tails first. Either the pins or tails are marked out and cut first, after which they are used directly as a template, to transfer the marking out on to the mating half of the joint. Transferring the locations of the tail and pin boundaries is done with a knife, an awl, a pencil or some such tool, as talked about in Chapter 2, Useful Techniques.

Traditional face-side and face-edge marks have been used, and the two parts have been prepared the same width and thickness, although this is not essential.

An engineer's try-square is used to check that joining ends are square to both face side and face edge, that the face side and face edge are prepared square to each other, and the opposite faces parallel to them.

First the thickness of the pinboard is gauged round the end of the tailboard, and the thickness of the tailboard is gauged on the face side and reverse face side of the pinboard, from their ends. I mark both boards lightly all round for simplicity, knowing that the markings can be planed off after assembly. These are the baselines, or shoulder lines, to which to cut the pins and tails.

### Tails First

With a bevel gauge set to 1:6, a slope suitable for most woods, gauge in the two sides of a tail on the tailboard, leaving space for a half-pin each side. The size of the half-pins should be approximately one eighth of the joint width.

Once marked, the sloped sides of the tail should be squared across the end of the tailboard, giving two lines to guide each saw cut. It can be seen in the photograph how I have also pencilled in the knife lines of the shoulders, which makes the limit of the saw cuts easier to see.

With the tailboard in the vise, or clamped securely to the bench, saw the corners away to leave the tail.

A marking gauge cuts a line into the face side of one of the parts. The line will be carried all round the end to define the baseline for a tailboard, or just on the reverse face side for a pinboard.

Using a bevel gauge when marking the slope of the tail. An ordinary HB pencil shows up clearly, but if the wood were dark then a white pencil would help.

Squaring the tail marking across the end of the tailboard completes the layout for the tail, ready for sawing.

Starting with the sloped cuts, concentrate initially at sawing a shallow kerf, square across the end grain, just sufficient to set the saw teeth into the wood enough to prevent the saw wandering. Then align the saw with the sloped line and saw down to the shoulder, without changing the tilt on the saw: don't worry if the saw doesn't exactly follow the layout line – it's far more important that these sloped cuts should be straight.

Some find these sloped cuts more easily sawn if the work is held so that the cuts are sawn vertically, rather than holding the saw at a slight tilt.

Reposition the tailboard in the vise lengthways, and saw the shoulder to release the waste section.

The saw will usually leave a remnant of waste right in the corner, between the tail side and the shoulder, which should be removed with a chisel (or knife). If the shoulder cut wasn't quite up to the knife line, then the waste should be pared back to the line before moving on.

With the tailboard completed it can be used as a template from which to mark the pinboard. Since the pins are marked directly from the prepared tailboard, any error made while sawing in the position or angle of the tail sides should be accounted for, except for that in how squarely across the end grain they were sawn.

Sawing the sloped tail sides with the work held vertically in the vise. You may find it easier to rotate the tailboard so that you saw vertically, rather than tilting the saw.

A saw cut on the waste side of the baseline, or shoulder, on the edge of the tailboard, will release the waste.

Using a sharp chisel to pare the scrap of waste left at the intersection of the two saw cuts, and any material proud of the baseline beside the tail.

The pinboard held in the vise while transferring the layout for the pins directly from the tailboard.

Similar to marking the tails, the sloped pin lines are squared round, only this time down the pinboard face as far as the shoulder line. This will be a guide for sawing square to the end of the board, and with time you may find it unnecessary, relying on clamping the pinboard vertically and naturally sawing plumb.

With these two pairs of lines the pin can be sawn, remembering to leave the line whilst sawing right up to it.

The pin sides are sawn down to the shoulder line, after which the waste is removed. In most cases I saw out the majority of the waste by dropping a coping saw or jeweller's saw down one kerf, almost to the shoulder line, and then rotating the blade whilst sawing so that it cuts across the bottom of the waste, just shy of the shoulder.

On rough work saw fully to the shoulder so that the tail will fit without further work. For finer work the remaining waste is chopped and pared with a chisel, working towards the middle of the board from each side to avoid breaking out the far side.

Using the try-square to mark the plumb cuts for the half-pins. These and the two sloped lines marked from the tail define the area of waste material between the half-pins.

Sawing the side of a half-pin, following the sloped line on the end grain and the plumb line on the face.

A coping saw removes the majority of waste between the half-pins. In some situations sawing right along the line will be satisfactory, whereas for finer work the line is left, and then a chisel is used to chop or pare to it.

Chopping the remaining waste up to the baseline, working from both sides.

Testing the fit before gluing the joint. The edges should be flush, with no gaps apparent, and the half-pins should not be forced apart.

Paring the socket flat, or very slightly concave, across the pinboard. A hump between baselines will prevent the joint from closing properly.

Ideally the joint will fit together with no gaps and without excessive force, and the two parts should have no movement between them, other than in the direction the joint goes together.

The half-pins should not be forced apart when the tail is inserted, as this risks the pin-board splitting, and if they are, then any excess material should be carefully pared from the pin sides until they are not.

Where a permanent connection is required the joint should be glued. Spread glue on the long grain surfaces of the pin sides and tail sides and assemble the joint. Excessive glue will make assembly more difficult and eventually squeeze out, so get used to how little is needed when joints are well fitted. Apply a little clamping pressure across the pins, and check that the tail is still fully seated against the pinboard baseline; also check that the two parts are at right angles.

**Pins First**

The joint can be prepared in a slightly different sequence, cutting the half-pins first and transferring the layout for the tail directly from the pinboard.

Shoulder lines are first scribed as before, but then the half-pins are marked out, starting with the sloped sides on the end grain. Remember that the thin end of the half-pins should be approximately one eighth of the width, and that they will be on the outside of the joint. These lines are then squared down to the shoulder line before sawing.

Remove the waste as before, and rest the pin-board on the inside face of the tailboard flush with the end; then scribe along the sides of the pins. Butting the parts up against a block will help keep them flush throughout scribing and reduce the risk of making a mistake.

Square the scribed marks of the tail sides across the end grain, and saw and fit the tail as before.

It doesn't take much glue to produce glue squeeze-out where the joint has been well prepared. This is the most I would like to see.

Using the completed pinboard as a template to mark in the tail using an awl.

The completed common dovetail: a big step towards understanding corner dovetails.

The scribed lines from the awl are clear to see. A retractable pencil or a slim scalpel blade would also do a fine job.

## THE DOVETAIL HALVING

The dovetail halving joins two boards in their width, and most commonly at right angles. Simple dovetail halvings use the full board width, showing the tail end grain on the far side, whereas lapped ones use a portion of the pinboard width to hide the end grain. Some examples are shown below.

Dovetail halvings are prepared tail first, creating the template for the socket. I shall describe the simple variant, but you will see that the others follow the same basic procedure.

### Initial Stock Preparation

The two parts should be carefully prepared, with each part having face side and face edge identified. As with other halving joints, gauging the half-way thickness for both parts is done from the face side, and the two face sides will be flush with each other when the joint is completed.

In preparing the stock, follow the guidelines below:

- Where the finished parts are to be flush both sides at the joint, they should be the same thickness.

A simple dovetail halving joint.

Both parts prepared square all round, of the same thickness, and with the joint end of the tailboard shot to 90 degrees. This will produce a tee joint at 90 degrees, with both faces flush.

Different versions of dovetail halvings (left to right): half tail, simple, lapped, gooseneck. Each is prepared by cutting the tail first, and using that as the template for the socket.

- Parts should be squared all round.
- The joining end of the tailboard should be prepared square to both the face side and face edge.

If it is desired that the boards do not join at a right angle, then the last guideline is partly ignored, with the end being shot at the desired angle to the face edge.

## Marking Out and Cutting

The width of the pinboard is marked all round the end of the tailboard, either directly or using a marking gauge.

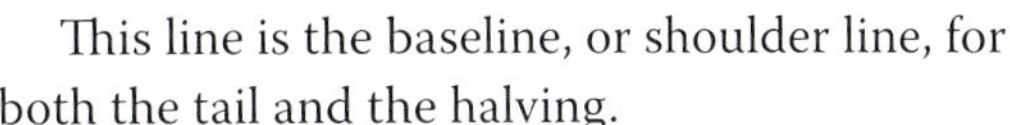

This line is the baseline, or shoulder line, for both the tail and the halving.

Using a marking gauge set to approximately half material thickness, mark the edges and end grain from the face side, round the end of the tailboard, meeting the baseline on both edges. Set the marking gauge aside for gauging the socket later on.

The slope of the tail should be between 1:5 and 1:8, and the neck of the tail should be at least two-thirds of the tailboard width. The tail can be marked in using a bevel gauge, or a ruler using construction marks on the wood itself.

Marking the baseline directly from the other part, using a backing block to keep the parts aligned.

The gauged line, clearly seen round the end of the board, will provide a positive reference to chop or pare to, after sawing.

Gauging the baseline, having set the gauge to the width of the other part.

A marking gauge set to half thickness gauges the halving line, defining the material to be removed behind the tail. The gauge setting is preserved for later on.

Using a bevel gauge to mark the sides of the tail, which should have a neck at least two-thirds the width of the tailboard.

Sawing the tail sides down to the baseline while keeping the cut square to the face side.

Once the tail and halving have been marked out, some cross-hatching of the waste to be removed is a good idea.

Sawing the halving cut on the tailboard, staying on the opposite side of the line to the face side.

## TAIL CONSIDERATIONS

For tailboards in softer woods, try to keep the slope to between 1:5 and 1:6. Since they are more easily compressed, the mechanical lock they provide is reduced. If the joining board is much wider than the tailboard, then use a half tail, or a lapped dovetail halving, to save the tail neck being too narrow and weak. If the joining board is much narrower than the tailboard, consider creating twin tails.

Saw the tail sides to the shoulder line, and then the halving cut on the reverse face side of the line, also to the shoulder line.

To separate the waste from the tailboard, three further saw cuts are made. The shoulders are sawn in from the edges to the neck of the tail, and from the baseline on the reverse of the face side.

All residual waste from the shoulders and the halving is then cleaned up with a sharp chisel, paring from the gauged lines. The flatness of the halving should be checked and corrected if necessary.

To mark for the dovetail socket, lay the tailboard in position with the halved tail over the face side of the joining board, and mark the two tail sides with a knife. These lines are squared round on to the edges and connected using the pre-set marking gauge, referenced from the face side.

After the waste from the sides of the tail has been sawn away, the final shoulder cut is made to release the waste from behind the tail.

Squaring the socket side lines round to the edges of the joining board with a try-square and marking knife.

With the tailboard in position, the sides of the tail can be transferred to the face side of the joining board, beginning the marking out for the dovetail socket.

The previously set marking gauge, referenced from the face side, is used to mark the halving lines for the socket at both the neck and top.

The extent of waste to be removed should be cross-hatched, ready for the socket to be prepared.

Working on the waste side of the socket lines, saw through to the halving point and then add extra relief cuts in the waste to the same depth.

Pare the waste away from the socket, working from each edge, and gradually down to the halving line. Because the halving line was gauged on both parts from the face side, when the tail and socket halvings are both prepared to the gauged lines, the assembled joint should be flush on the surface. Using a router plane is a

Preparing the socket, starting with sawing halfway through against the marking lines for the dovetail sides.

Paring the waste down to the halfway point, which can be seen a little below the chisel. Notice the chisel just fits between additional relief cuts, making the task more controlled and easier.

The joint, part assembled without glue, shows the close-fitting joint lines, and how it won't simply fall into place. This fit gives the joint a lot of strength, even before it is glued.

very easy way to finish the removal of waste to the correct depth, planing in from each edge to avoid any breakout.

Complete the socket by paring the sides to the knife lines transferred from the tail. A friction fit with no slop is key to giving the joint maximum mechanical strength.

When dry fitted, the two parts should go together and lie flush with each other.

To glue the joint, apply glue to all three surfaces in the socket and to the underside of the

## TAIL TROUBLE

### Tail Too Tight

If the tail appears too tight, there are two possible reasons, one or both of which may need to be addressed. First, check that the top of the tail does in fact reach the top of the socket. If not, then the shoulders of the tail and halving need attention. Possibly there is still some waste left in a corner, or maybe the shoulder line hasn't been marked or pared to quite correctly. Correct for this first, but do so gradually as it is better to have the tail slightly short rather than loose.

The other reason could be that the tail and socket are not quite matched. Maybe the sides of the tail or socket haven't been prepared square to the face side, or perhaps when tracing the socket from the tail the knife was undercutting a little. Correct for squareness first, before reducing the tail width if necessary. Removing too much will result in a loose fit, when the desired wedging action and mechanical strength is lost.

### Tail Too Loose

To fix a tail that is loose due to being longer than the width of the joining board, glue a short strip of veneer to the face-edge side of the joining board, building it up across the socket to the length of the tail. Extend the socket through the veneer, and plane it down until the tail fits.

For a tail that is simply too narrow, glue strips of veneer to one or both sides as necessary, and pare back to fit.

### Tail Not Flush with the Joining Board

This problem is due to the halving not being marked or cut correctly. If the tail is proud of the joining board, then remove more material from the mating faces of the halving, until the parts become flush.

If the tail is shy of the joining board, then glue veneers to the mating faces, and once dry, pare back for a flush fit.

tail. This will avoid scraping glue off the sides of the tail as it is inserted.

The long-grain to long-grain surfaces should be kept in close contact while the glue cures, so clamp across the joint using waxed cauls to spread the pressure.

If the finished joint is prepared well it should require virtually no planing or sanding to flush the surfaces off. Any layout or other markings can be dealt with using a smoothing plane or card scraper.

The variations on the dovetail halving shown earlier in the chapter should not be beyond your capabilities once you manage this one, and you will recognise similarities in preparation with some of the joints shown in Chapter 5.

Glue applied to the socket and tail. The long-grain to long-grain glue surface of the halving gives a lot of strength to the joint, so long as these surfaces are in good contact with each other.

Waxed cauls spread the clamping pressure evenly across the whole joint, and the well fitted dovetail prevents the joint from slipping out of alignment.

## THE THROUGH DOVETAIL

The through dovetail is without doubt the joint that most people associate with dovetails, and with so much of the joint being visible it is certainly a test of basic layout and cutting accuracy.

Essentially the joint is a multiple common dovetail, which might mislead the beginner as to how easy it is to make. The multiple tails

The completed dovetail halving. A light pass with a smoothing plane will remove the face-side marks, while a card scraper or sandpaper will remove the face-edge marks.

Most people think of the through dovetail when they hear dovetail joint. It has been widely used for jointing strong chests and the backs of drawers for centuries.

## ONE OF MANY

Recognised by virtually all woodworkers and many non-woodworkers, the through dovetail is seen as the first choice for constructing strong, long-lasting corner joints, joints that will often function long after any glue has perished.

However, the through dovetail is strictly one type of many through dovetails, the others having names that either end in *through dovetail*, or even omit the *through* completely. The overriding rule is that these dovetail joints have the ends of the pins and tails exposed through the tailboard and pinboard respectively. Many more will be described later in the book.

There are other through dovetails, but only the simple, plain form is known as *the* through dovetail joint.

restrict access when transferring layout and removing waste material, and adjusting the fit of one pin or tail can throw out the alignment of its neighbours.

Nevertheless it is still relatively easy, and I shall cover its preparation in detail. As a demonstration I shall make a simple cabinet maker's through dovetail in contrasting timber.

Two boards prepared ready to make a through dovetail, as the one behind. The dovetail marking gauge will be used to mark the slope of the tails.

## Initial Stock Preparation

The two parts, the tailboard and pinboard, should be carefully prepared. All four long-grain faces are flat, squared to their neighbours (squared all round) and with their ends shot square.

Face-side and face-edge marking should be used, and the specific ends to be joined identified in order to avoid ending up with the boards connected the wrong way round. This does happen, although usually just once in a woodworker's life.

You may notice that the boards are the same width. This is not essential, and where different widths are used it will be helpful to provide an index on the ends, such that they can be quickly and accurately aligned when the layout is transferred from one to the other.

Also notice that the boards are different thicknesses, which is very common and makes no appreciable difference to the method of preparation. A good example is with drawer construction, where the drawer front is thick but the sides are thinner to maximise drawer capacity and save material and weight.

## Marking Out and Cutting

As with the common dovetail, there are two orders in which the joint can be marked out, known as pins first or tails first. With the only difference essentially being which part is used as the template to transfer the joint layout to the other, I shall describe the method of preparation in the tails first order.

The width of the tailboard is marked on both sides of the pinboard, and that of the pinboard is marked on both sides and edges, right round the end of the tailboard, using a marking gauge.

Working tails first, the two half-pins are gauged from the edges of the tailboard.

Next the tails are spaced between these half-pins, in this case two equal tails with a narrow gap between them, in simple cabinet-maker style. The exact positions for the tails are stepped off across the board with the spring dividers.

A one-in-eight slope is ideal for the hardwood being used here. In softwood, a one-in-five or one-in-six slope would be better.

When marking the tails, if your dovetail marking gauge includes a square edge, place the pencil tip in the divots left by the dividers and slide the gauge up against it. Otherwise line up the top of the gauge slope with lines squared across from the divots. The divots will disappear when the tails or pins are sawn.

Saw the sides of the tails down to the baseline. If you find it easier, angle the tailboard to match the slope of all the left-hand sides and cut these first, before matching the slope of the right-hand sides and cutting them. Sawing well with the saw tilted takes a little practice, but avoids all the repositioning.

Importantly, follow the squared lines across the end of the board to ensure that the layout

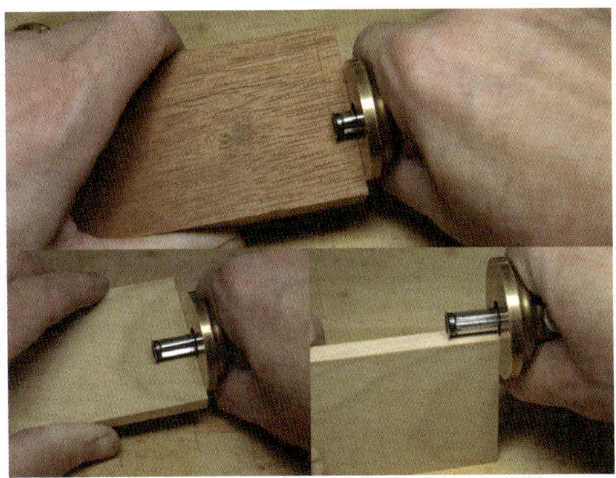

Marking out starts with gauging the thickness of the tailboard to the pinboard, and vice versa. The pinboard is only marked across its width.

The width of the half-pin being marked with a pair of spring dividers. The opposing half-pin need not be the same width.

Marking in the tails with the 1:8 dovetail gauge. This gauge includes a square edge that can also mark the top of the tails.

## STEPPING-OFF TAILS OR PINS WITH DIVIDERS

Decide on the width of the half-pins, and mark this on the board. These half-pins do not need to be identical in width, a point that many tutorials seem to miss out. Size them to suit what you are doing. I shall continue as if talking about tails on a tailboard, then explain the only difference when marking a pinboard.

With half-pins defined on each side on the end of the tailboard, the dividers are used to determine the spacing for the tails.

1. Choose how many tails you desire, and set the divider to approximately that fraction of the distance between the half-pin marks.
2. Set one leg of the dividers on the left-hand half-pin mark, and swing the other leg as far to the right as it will go. Count zero.
3. Prick the right-hand leg lightly into the board and swing the other leg round to the right. Add one to the count.
4. Repeat the last step until the divider passes the right-hand half-pin mark. Hopefully your count has reached the desired number of tails. If not, then reduce the divider gap to increase the count, or widen the gap to reduce the count, and start again from step 2.
5. The distance that the divider leg falls short of the right-hand half-pin mark equals the intermediate gap between tails. Small adjustments to the divider gap can be made to get this intermediate gap to the size you like (starting from step 2 each time).
6. Starting at the left-hand half-pin, step off the desired number of tails, pricking each point along the way enough to create a permanent divot.
7. Set the divider on the right-hand half-pin mark, and step off the desired number of tails, towards the left, leaving divots again.
8. Use a try-square and pencil to mark across the tailboard end in line with each divot.
9. Use a dovetail marking gauge to drop tail sides down from the lines to the baseline, to complete the layout.

For a pinboard, step 9 is changed so that the dovetail marking gauge is placed to mark its sloped lines across the end of the board, defining the dovetail shaped waste areas. Then the ends of the sloped lines are squared down to the baseline.

If you are comfortable cutting with the saw tilted, then all the tails can be cut without having to reset the tailboard in the vise.

can be accurately transferred to the pinboard and the pins can be cut plumb. Don't try to correct a slight run-off from the sloped line, but rather keep the cut straight.

After the sides are cut the waste between the tails can be mostly removed by using a jeweller's saw or similar. For carpenter's dovetails, the wider waste is usually chopped out for speed, in what is often a softwood.

The waste from the outside of the tails is sawn next. To protect the joint shoulders a chisel is used to pare down to the base of the gauged line from the waste side. This reveals a knife wall against which the saw teeth can be positioned when starting the cut to the base of the tail.

When the saw cuts are made, attention is given to preserving the baseline and stopping the cut before going into the tail. Essential to this is keeping the saw plumb to the work in both directions; this is most easily done with the tailboard held horizontally in a vise.

The shoulder cuts are pared down to the baseline, making sure to remove any material left where the intersecting saw cuts meet.

With both the shoulders prepared, attention is turned to the waste left between the tails. In cabinet-maker's dovetails these areas are usually very tight and a narrow chisel will be used. Little force is required to pare the waste with such a chisel, and so it should be pinched up close to the tip such that it only reaches about two-thirds of the way across, preventing it from possibly damaging the opposite edge.

Paring needs to be done from both sides, so first start all the gaps from one side, then reverse the board and complete them.

A final check of the tailboard should be made to ensure that both shoulders and

A fine jeweller's saw can easily and cleanly remove most of the waste between the tails, which in cabinet maker's dovetails can often be more difficult to chop out without damage to the surrounding material.

The saw is stopped as soon as the half-pin waste is freed, to prevent damage to the tail.

Having gauged the baseline all round the tailboard, it is possible to pare into it to create a protective knife wall for the saw cut that comes next.

Having preserved the crisp edges left by the marking gauge, a final paring cut is used to level the shoulder, and to clear any remaining waste from within the corner.

all gaps between tails are square to the face side, and have no high spots or waste remaining that would prevent the joint assembling nicely.

To transfer the layout to the pinboard, it is held vertically in the vise, extending above by the height of a spacer, quite commonly a bench plane on its side.

The spacer is moved back by a hand span and the tailboard used to bridge the gap, aligning the joint ends such that the shoulder line of the tailboard is tight to the rear side of the pinboard.

A light source, either shone or placed beneath the tailboard, will only just appear through the tailboard shoulders and the gaps between tails.

Exert pressure down on the tailboard with one hand to prevent it moving, while the tails are used as a template to copy the layout with a knife into the end of the pinboard using the other hand.

Pinching the chisel to prevent it pushing right through to the far side, as the waste between the tails is pared down to the baseline.

A pinboard set vertically in the vise, at the same height as, in this case, a practice joint. Frequently a bench plane resting on its side is used as a spacer for convenience.

Checking that the shoulders and between the tails are square, and that there are no humps, to ensure the joint will assemble well.

A tailboard resting between a spacer and its prospective pinboard can be positioned easily to use as a layout template.

In carpenter's dovetails there is often enough space to use a pencil to transfer the layout, in which case the thickness of the lines marked will be within the material to be retained as pins. Not accounting for this will result in a loose joint. Using a knife should leave a vertical wall to cut to, with a little compressed area where the bevel of the knife was drawn through.

The pin layout on the end grain is next squared down to the baseline, and the waste clearly identified ready for sawing.

Clearly visible, the knifed layout of pin ends is ready to be augmented with vertical guide lines down the face side.

Aligning the tailboard atop the pinboard, using light from underneath to fix the baseline, and sighting the edges.

Plumb lines being marked in from the pin layout to the baseline with a try-square and pencil.

Knifing round the tails to transfer the layout whilst holding the tailboard hard down to the pinboard end. The slim scalpel is sometimes the only knife that will fit when the gap between tails is very narrow.

For extra contrast on the dark wood, a white pencil has been used to define the waste areas to be removed from the pinboard.

Now it is time to cut the pins, and in order to achieve a tight fit the saw should cut up to the line, and not bisect it. Starting exactly up to the line can be simplified for the beginner by paring a knife wall against the layout lines, although with a little sawing experience this should become redundant.

The pin sides are sawn down to the shoulder line, and then a jeweller's saw or similar used to remove the bulk of the waste material.

Remember the pins are sloped and that you need to swing the angle of the jeweller's saw during the cut to avoid cutting into them.

Paring from both baselines, the remaining area between the pins is levelled. Remember to pinch the chisel for control. I find I can work more quickly with a narrower chisel than might seem appropriate to the width of the gap. Experiment to find what works best for you.

As with the tailboard, waste should be fully removed to the baseline so that no high spots remain. A small router plane, or some wheel-making gauges, can be used to check for and remove these in one operation.

The fit should be tested before gluing the joint and adjusted if necessary so that the

If you find it hard to start the saw precisely against the layout lines, create knife walls by paring from the waste into the bottom of the lines.

The jeweller's saw has to be angled, first one way then the other, to avoid cutting into the pins when sawing out the waste.

Sawing the sides of the pins, keeping the saw kerf in the waste.

Paring back to the baseline from the jeweller's saw cut. The aim is to connect the baselines on both sides with a flat surface.

half-pins are not forced apart as it is assembled. The difference between too tight and too loose isn't very large, so go slowly.

Close inspection of the pins should reveal any sides that require further trimming to the layout line. If it is unclear, set up the boards as if to transfer the layout again, and look where light is totally obscured. Address the pins by paring across the grain, working from both sides.

When the fit is good, a little glue is applied to the sides of the pins and tails before final assembly.

Once glued and assembled, the joint should be checked and adjusted if necessary to ensure it is absolutely square before allowing the glue to cure.

A well fitted joint should not require clamping unless it is stressed at all. In practical situations, such as drawer-box construction where a frame is glued up together, some stress will almost certainly be involved and clamps should be used to hold the whole assembly in true.

If clamps are required to hold the tailboard tight against the pinboard, possibly because the tailboard has cupped a little, then prepare some MDF cauls to fit the tails so that the pins are not compressed.

Checking that the bottom of the sockets are free from high spots with a wheel-style marking gauge. Any high spots are easily removed with the wheel's sharp cutting edge.

Tight spots can be pared across the grain, removing a small amount at a time and re-testing.

Assembling the joint without glue to check the fit, making sure that the half-pins are not being deflected. Lighting from behind can be used to pinpoint areas that need adjustment.

Just a small amount of glue is required so long as the joint fits well. A similar amount on the sides of the tails will be more than enough.

Checking that the glued and assembled joint is square before leaving it to cure. Minor discrepancies can be overcome easily, but some clamping may be required.

The completed through dovetail joint. Because of the narrow gap between the tails, this particular joint could only be prepared by hand.

## PRACTISE BOTH ORDERS

When practising, I suggest you prepare three boards and start with the 'tails first' method. Mark out the tails and cut them, and then transfer the layout from the tailboard to the second board, ready to cut matching pins. Once the pins have been cut, use them to transfer the layout to the third board, and cut a second tailboard. The two tailboards should be identical, and a good fit to the pinboard.

Now cut off the pins and tails and repeat the process, only starting by laying out a pinboard first, and going from there.

## THE LAPPED DOVETAIL

The lapped dovetail is the discrete brother of the through dovetail. Functionally the same, it hides its presence from all but one direction, making it an obvious choice for attaching drawer fronts to sides, without interrupting the show face. With much of the joint being hidden, appearance is less of a testament to accurate preparation.

Essentially, the joint is a through dovetail that doesn't quite make it all the way through the pinboard. In fact lapped dovetail joints can be created from through dovetails by

A lapped dovetail joint, as might be found at the front of a drawer box where the secondary wood used for the sides should not be seen unless the drawer is open.

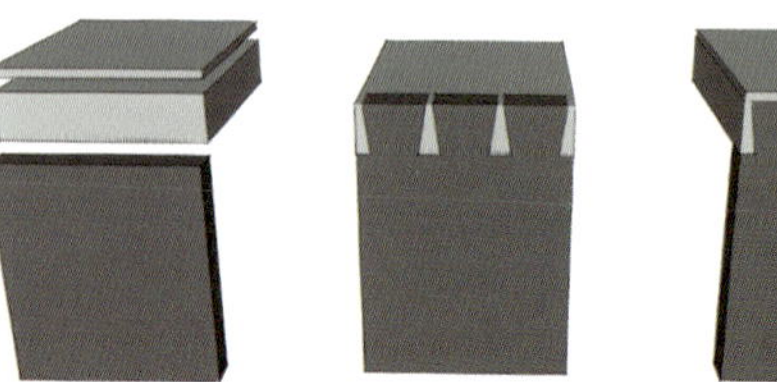

A lapped dovetail can be constructed by first through dovetailing and then laminating a thin facing to the pinboard, preferably previously ripped from the pinboard so that the grain and figure match well.

gluing a previously ripped-off face back on to the pinboard.

As for the previous through dovetail, in this example the tailboard will be significantly thinner than the pinboard. This is not a rule but is usually so with drawer construction. In case construction the tailboard and pinboard will usually be a similar thickness.

## Initial Stock Preparation

The tailboard and pinboard should be prepared with all four long-grain faces flat, squared all round and with the ends shot square.

You should now be in the habit of using face-side and face-edge marking, and identifying the specific ends to be joined.

## Marking Out and Cutting

The width of the tailboard is marked on the inside of the pinboard, leaving the front unmarked. This defines the depth to which the sockets need to be cut in order for the tailboard to finish flush when assembled.

A lap line is marked, using a marking gauge from the rear of the pinboard, across the end.

Without changing the marking gauge setting, this same distance is marked right round the end of the tailboard, ensuring that the tail baseline lines up with the rear of the pinboard.

### EXPLAINING LAP

The lap is the distance from this line to the face of the pinboard, or in other words, by how much the tails are held back from the front of the joint. The lap should be sufficiently wide to prevent the ends of the tails ghosting through, either due to high colour contrast or the tails deforming the face of the pinboard if it contracts in a dry atmosphere. From my experience 3mm has always been safe.

Marking gauge set to the thickness of the pinboard, minus the lap. In most cases I set a minimum lap of 3mm, so that the appearance of the front of the pinboard is always preserved.

Gauging the baseline on the rear only of the pinboard. Since the tails don't extend through to the front, the baseline isn't needed there.

The tailboard baseline is marked so that the tails will reach the lap line of the pinboard.

As with through dovetails you can choose whether to cut lapped dovetails pins first or tails first.

**Pins First**

Divide the pinboard end as described for the through dovetail, and then use the divisions to align a dovetail marking gauge, or a bevel gauge, and mark in the tail-shaped sockets between the lap line and the rear of the pinboard.

Extend lines from the socket layout on the end grain, down to the baseline, mark in the waste to be removed, and saw the socket sides. Because of the lap, sawing these sides is limited to a diagonal between the lap line and the baseline.

The socket waste is chopped out, working across the grain, starting close to the end and gradually moving towards the baseline. Ignore the sloped sides of the sockets for now, and keep the chisel plumb to the board; angling the chisel makes it harder to control the depth that the chisel reaches. You can use marker pen or masking tape applied to the chisel to define a maximum depth of cut, just shy of the lap line. After the first cut is made to depth, during subsequent chops you should hear a noticeable change in tone once the correct depth is reached.

After the baseline has been reached, use a chisel to pare the sides and rear of the sockets to the layout lines, keeping the cuts square at all times. The waste in the corners is best tackled with multiple thin cuts, rather than trying to punch out the whole amount in one go.

Skew chisels will allow cutting right into the rear corners, or if not available, use a narrow chisel to get as close as possible, and then a pointed knife.

After deciding on the layout, the sockets are marked out on the end of the pinboard using a dovetail marking gauge.

When sawing the sides of the sockets in the pinboard, it is only possible to cut down to the diagonal between the lap line and the baseline.

Chopping out the waste between the pins, being careful to go only as deep as the lap.

Having prepared the pinboard, it can be held in position over the tailboard, aligned with the edges and the baseline, to allow the layout to be transferred. In small work, such as this example, a slim scalpel blade is ideal for the task, whereas in larger work awls or pencils will also work fine.

The tails can then be cut in the usual way and fitted to the pins.

### Tails First

The tailboard end is divided and marked out for tails in the same way as for through dovetails.

The tails are cut and waste material removed as for through dovetails. When

A slim scalpel transfers the layout from the pinboard to the tailboard. The thinner the tailboard is, the more challenging the access.

Paring the flare of the sockets, by gradually parting the long-grain fibres, keeping the chisel back square to the base.

Tails laid out and marked with spring dividers and dovetail marking gauge, in the 'tails first' method.

Slicing the bottom of parted long-grain fibres along the side and rear of the socket, here using a skew chisel, although a scalpel is also a good choice.

After cutting the tails, they should just reach the lap line on the pinboard.

completed, and the shoulders aligned with the rear of the pinboard, the tails should reach the lap line.

Holding the tailboard tight to and aligned to the pinboard, the sides of the tails are used to guide a knife as the layout is transferred into the end grain.

Lines are squared down to the baseline and the waste material clearly marked before the sockets are cut the same way as for the 'pins first' method.

Once the fit is good, glue is applied to the sides of the pins before assembly. Immediately after gluing the joint should be checked and adjusted if necessary so it is absolutely square.

The same clamping guidance applies as for through dovetails. Clamp only if necessary to keep it square, or remove the cup from the boards and use appropriate cauls for protection.

Don't hang up your apron just yet – there are plenty of other dovetail joints to try, starting with more corner joints in the next chapter.

Scribing in the sockets on the pinboard, using the tailboard as a template. The white paper reflects light up to the baseline of the tailboard to help alignment.

In lapped dovetail preparation, skew chisels allow access right up into the acute corners of sockets.

The scribed sides of the pins, together with the lap line, define the shape of the socket to be cut, and the waste should be clearly marked. As the sides of the sockets are cut on a diagonal, the board must sit quite high in the vise.

The completed lapped dovetail joint. You can't tell whether this was the 'pins first' or 'tails first' method, and that's the way it should be.

## THE MECHANICS OF WOODEN DOVETAILS: PART 1

### Geometry

Like a finger joint, the interlocking pins and tails of the dovetail prevent displacement of parts along the joint line. In addition, the trapezoidal shape of the pins and tails prevents displacement of parts across the joint line in the tailboard plane. In order for the joint to be assembled, the parts can slide together and apart in the pinboard plane.

The dovetail joint geometry makes it a suitable choice for drawer construction. Under normal circumstances there is very limited force pushing the sides of a drawer away from each other, and sideways away from the front or back. However, there is regular force pulling the drawer fronts away from the sides and back, whenever the drawer is opened. Plus, the inertia of items within the drawer will exert pressure on the back when opening. Therefore it makes sense to have pinboards for the front and back of a drawer, and tailboards for the sides.

The trapezoidal shape of dovetail pins and tails resolves a pulling apart force into two forces, one trying to separate the parts in the direction of the tailboard length, and the other compressing the tails and pins across the joint. Any compression of tails and pins allows the joint to be partially opened, and given sufficient compression the two parts could be completely separated. Designing for this is covered in The Mechanics of Wooden Dovetails: Part 2, at the end of the next chapter.

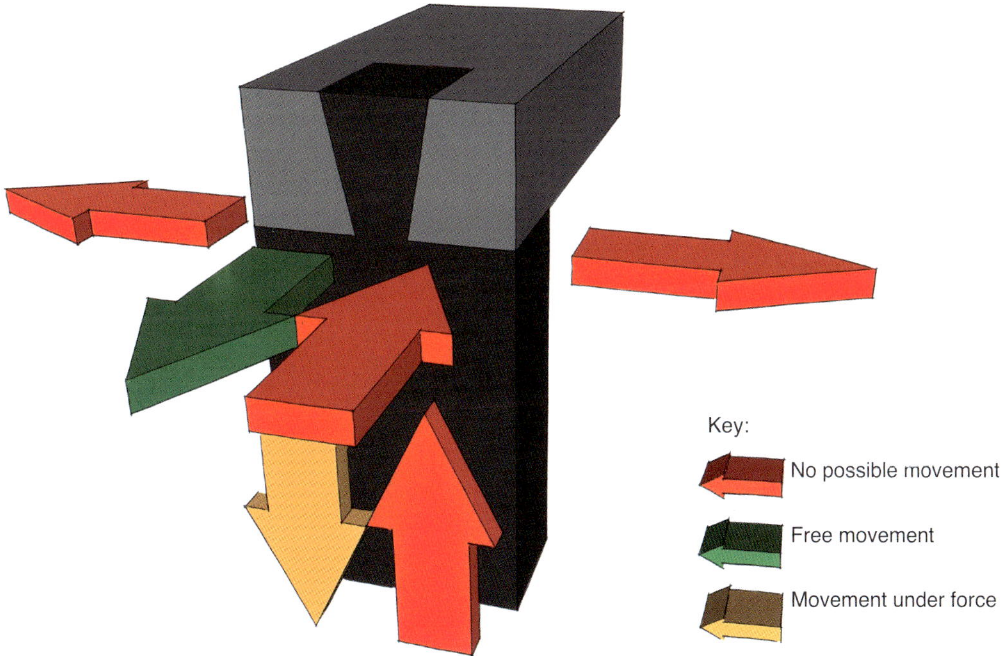


The freedom of movement of an unglued tailboard in a dovetail joint.

CHAPTER 4

# CORNER JOINTS

Having already covered the best known and most used dovetail joints for corners, you might ask what is left for a chapter dedicated to corner joints. The answer, simply, is lots.

Such is the usefulness of the dovetail ability to mechanically hold parts together, a whole host of variations has been spawned, some for practical purposes – for example to tackle joining boards at angles other than 90 degrees – and some purely for aesthetic reasons. A good example of the latter is the secret mitre dovetail, where the function of the dovetail is maintained while the appearance of it is completely hidden from view.

I certainly can't claim to include all the many variations there might be, but I shall cover all those that I've used over the years, ones that I have tried for the sake of it, and even ones I have never seen elsewhere.

Some of the joints in this chapter are in regular use today, while others are used far less frequently, but all of them function and offer the woodworker options when designing items.

## ACUTE- AND OBTUSE-ANGLE DOVETAILS

Most dovetail corner joints will be made at 90 degrees, but occasionally acute or obtuse angled joints are desired. Preparation of these follow much the same procedure, with just a few differences, explained below.

Examples of acute and obtuse dovetails. Although most joints will be at 90 degrees, knowing how to break away from that might come in useful.

### Initial Stock Preparation

In preparing the stock, most of the guidelines are the same as before, with the exception of the ends of the boards to be jointed:

- Where the finished parts are to be flush at the joint, they should be the same width.
- The thickness of joint parts can be different, but each part should have a consistent thickness.
- Parts should be square all round.

The many dovetail corner joints covered in Chapter 4.

- The ends should be prepared square to the edges.
- The ends should be prepared at the angle the joint is designed to be with the face sides.

A shooting board with an auxiliary wedge is most useful for preparing the angle on the board ends. The board rests on the wedge and against the standard shooting-board fence, and is shot with the plane in the usual way.

Preparing the ends to the desired final shape simplifies joint layout, and will be revisited when we look at bevelled dovetails.

## Marking Out and Cutting

First the bevel length of the pinboard is marked round the end of the tailboard, and the bevel length of the tailboard is marked on the face side and reverse face side of the pinboard, from their ends. Depending on whether the joint angle is acute or obtuse, marking one of the faces is impossible with a marking gauge so these should be marked with a try-square, lining up from each edge marking.

### Tails First

The tails are marked on the tailboard, following the previous guidance on tail spacing and layout. The sides of the tails are sawn next, taking particular care not to cross the baselines. (Marking the tails on the acute side means that you can always saw horizontally, with the board vertical in the vise, without the risk of cutting

## CLOSED DOVETAILED FRAMES

Careful thought needs to be given when designing closed frames with dovetails, especially those including non 90-degree corners. Just because a closed frame can be drafted, it does not follow that the component parts can be assembled, and where they can, there may be a specific order in which assembly must take place.

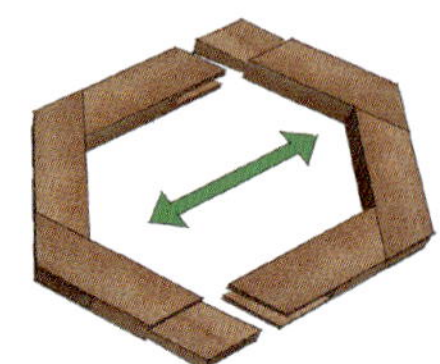

A dovetailed pentagon can't be assembled with identical corner joints, but a hexagon can. When designing a frame, just because it can exist, doesn't mean it can be assembled.

Regular odd-sided frames such as pentagons cannot have identical dovetail joints, at least not without quite a few sides and some brute force. However, even-sided frames can, as it is possible to slide two halves of the frame together easily.

The ends of the pinboard and tailboard have been sawn and shot at the same angle as that of the finished joint. A standard shooting board with an add-on ramp makes this task an easy one.

below the opposite baseline.) Saw, chop, and pare away all the waste around the tails.

With the tailboard completed it can be used as a template from which to mark the pinboard, just as with right-angled dovetail joints.

Square the pin lines down the pinboard face side, as far as the baseline. You can use a try-square for acute joint angles, as the stock will register fine on the angled edge. For obtuse angles a pencil gauge registered from the face edge is easier, as the try-square stock will be hard to register on the bevelled end.

Next the pins are sawn, again being careful to stop at the offset baselines.

Remove all the waste between the pins, and ideally the joint will fit together with no gaps and without excessive force. Remember that it goes together with the boards angled to each other, and not square.

**Pins First**

These joints can be prepared pins first, however it can become very difficult to transfer the layout for acute lapped dovetails, as the angle gets smaller.

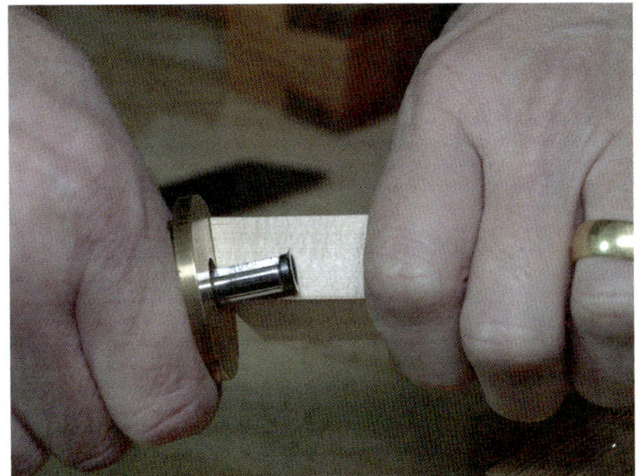

Gauging the baseline on a tailboard, using a marking gauge set to the width of the bevel prepared on the end of the pinboard, and then marking the baseline between the edge marks, using a try-square. Marking gauges cannot be used accurately from the bevelled end.

The tails and waste clearly marked out, with the spacing and layout the same as that for regular through dovetails. When clearing the waste, remember that the shoulders are angled and check them with the bevel gauge for high spots.

Holding the parts aligned for transferring the layout is more of a challenge when the joint is not at 90 degrees, especially when they are particularly long or wide.

Try-squares are hard to control on bevelled ends, so a pencil gauge is useful to extend pin lines accurately to the baseline.

Gluing is the same as for right-angled dovetails, but as the angle gets further away from 90 degrees, knocking and clamping joints together can be awkward. Attaching temporary glue blocks to the pinboard can allow clamps to pull the joints together, without also forcing the joint out of alignment.

## THE BEVELLED (SLOPING) DOVETAIL

In some cases, one part of a joint may want to slope, perhaps the handled sides of a tray, for example. It would be useful if the functionality of a dovetail joint could be adapted to such circumstances. Preparation of the bevelled or sloping dovetail joint is very similar to joints without a sloping part, except that care should be taken in laying out the tail angles.

As the slope angle increases, the tails marked with a dovetail marking gauge will be rotated in relation to the tailboard grain direction. Consequently the tails become weaker and more liable to fail. A stronger and more pleasing layout is achieved by angling the tails as though the end of the tailboard were square to the sides.

Sawing the pins while remembering that the baselines are offset due to the angle.

The bevelled or sloping dovetail, where one side is out of plumb.

## Initial Stock Preparation

In preparing the stock, exceptions to the normal guidelines are as follows:

- Sloping boards should be made pinboards, and have their edges planed so that they lie in the same plane as the edges of the upright tailboards. Importantly, this means the pinboards need to be prepared from wider stock than the tailboards, assuming that the parts should be flush top and bottom.
- Upright boards will be tailboards, and should have their ends angled to match the slope of the pinboards.

Rest the boards on edge on a flat bench, in the position the joint goes together, to check that the pinboard edges are planed correctly, and that both boards are the correct width.

An imaginary tray with upright front and back sides, and sloping handle sides. Clearly the strength of dovetail joints is desirable here.

In bevelled dovetails, tails marked with a gauge (left) look odd and are weakened, so angle them as if the end were plumb (right).

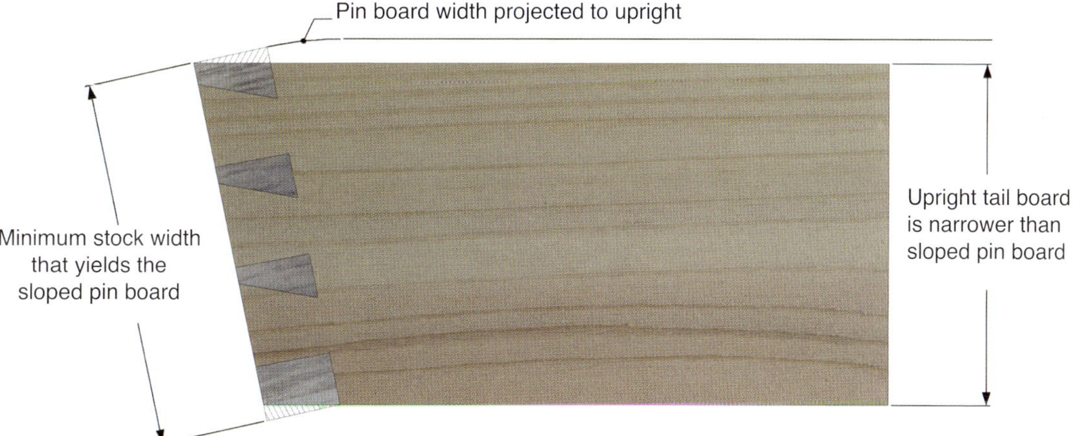


The true width of the sloping pinboard is greater than that of the tailboard, where their finished edges are to be flush to each other.

## Marking Out and Cutting

The thickness of the tailboard is gauged across the front and rear of the pinboard end. The thickness of the pinboard is marked round the end of the tailboard, either directly or using a marking gauge, giving the dovetail baseline. Due to the angled end, a try-square is used to connect the baseline across the edges of the board.

Using the true width of the tailboard, rather than the slope length of the end, allow for half-pins and space-tails as for a normal through dovetail. Carry the divisions, parallel to the edges, along to the sloped end, and square them across.

Now use a bevel gauge to mark the tail sides at the desired slope, say 1:6. The bevel gauge should be referenced from the end when setting it, marking six units up one of the division lines and one unit square to the edge of the board.

After cutting the tails in the normal way, the tailboard can then be used to transfer the layout directly to the pinboard.

The sides of the pins are then squared down the pinboard, to meet a baseline gauged across the front and rear, and the pins cut as normal.

A try-square is used to mark the baseline across the edges of the tailboard, after the sides have been marked with a marking gauge set to the pinboard thickness.

Transferring the layout from the angled tailboard to the sloped pinboard, by using it as a guide to knife round.

Tails are spaced across the width of the tailboard, not along the sloped end, and carried along to the end, before tail sides are marked in using a bevel gauge referenced to the edges.

Test-fitting the prepared joint, prior to gluing up. Judicious paring may be needed to achieve a well fitted joint that isn't too tight.

Once the pins and tails have been cleaned up, the two boards should fit together. As with other joints, a little fitting may be required to achieve a slip fit suitable for gluing. However, be careful that the bevelled angle at which they should be assembled doesn't cloud your judgement as to where any further paring needs to take place.

The bevel dovetail really isn't that much more complicated than a simple through dovetail, unlike the next joint.

Using some of the previous preparation techniques, you should be able to attempt lapped obtuse, and lapped bevel dovetails, and begin to predict, in part, how future dovetails are prepared. Experience of these will considerably help your woodworking progress.

The double-bevel (oblique) dovetail, perhaps the hardest dovetail joint I have ever encountered.

## THE DOUBLE-BEVEL (OBLIQUE) DOVETAIL

For me, the double-bevel dovetail is one of the most difficult to prepare, and requires either a pre-prepared table of angles, or angles to be found by direct projection, drawing projection, 3D modelling, or trigonometry. However, I will demonstrate the simplest method that works remarkably well, and has no prerequisites other than some basic dexterity. I will also include details on the more complex and arguably more accurate methods.

### The Four Methods

As an example we will use a hopper, 300 × 300 × 100mm (12 × 12 × 4in), with 25mm (1in)-thick walls tilted at 45 degrees.

#### Direct Projection

The simplest method, albeit open to operator error, is to build the joint by transferring layout lines from one side to the other using direct projection of their surface planes.

The two sides are angled at the desired slope(s) and aligned at right angles to each other, and a U-shaped board is used to project the intersecting planes from one to the other.

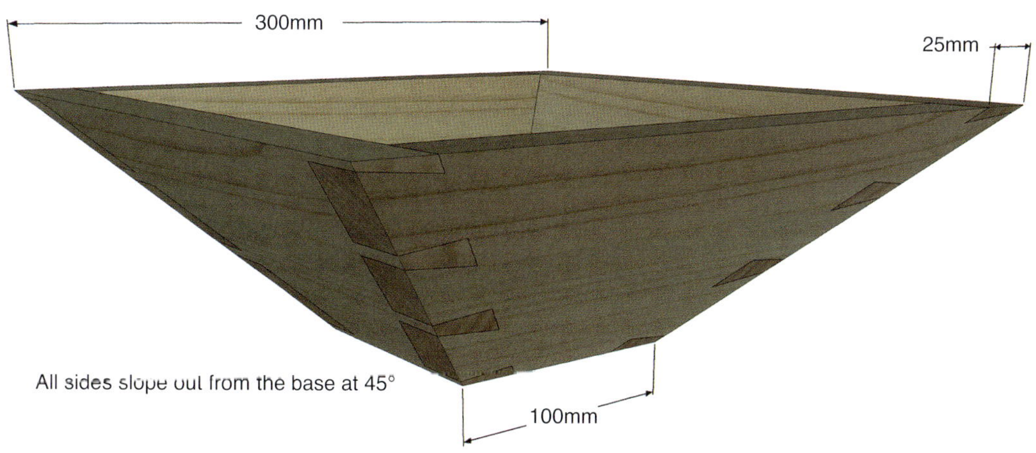


A hopper with dovetail corner joints. I inserted a base after making this, turning it into a fruit bowl.

Using a piece of MDF with a cut-out: the inner and outer surfaces of one board can be projected on to the inner and outer surfaces of the other.

Scribing where the outer surface projection of one board intersects the inner surface of the other.

Both inside and outside surfaces are scribed, for both boards: when joined across the edges, this gives the compound cut lines and dovetail baselines.

Holding the parts together in alignment, without moving, whilst projecting and scribing all these lines, is quite a challenge.

**Drawing Projection**

A scale drawing showing both elevation and plan view are prepared, and by projecting the true side dimensions from the elevation into the plan the true mitre angle can be ascertained. The board thickness, cast across the projected side mitre, gives the mitre bevel angle.

It is also possible to determine that the length of each side, before the edges are bevelled, mitres cut, and mitres bevelled, is longer than might be expected.

**Trigonometry**

Having found no trigonometric solutions from any sources, I developed the following myself, which will solve where all sides tilt at the same angle. The standard inputs are the tilt of the sides from vertical (ts), the finish height (h), and the bevel width (bw).

With these formulae, rearranged if necessary, a double-bevel dovetail joint design can

$$\text{Board Thickness, } b = bw(\cos(ts))$$

$$\text{Board Width, } w = \frac{h}{\cos(ts)} + (b \times \tan(ts))$$

$$\text{Edge Bevel Angle} = 90^\circ - ts$$

$$\text{True Mitre Angle, } Mt = \tan^{-1}\left(\frac{1}{\cos(ts) \times \tan(ts)}\right)$$

$$\text{True Mitre Bevel, } Mb = \tan^{-1}(\cos(Mt) \times \tan(ts)$$

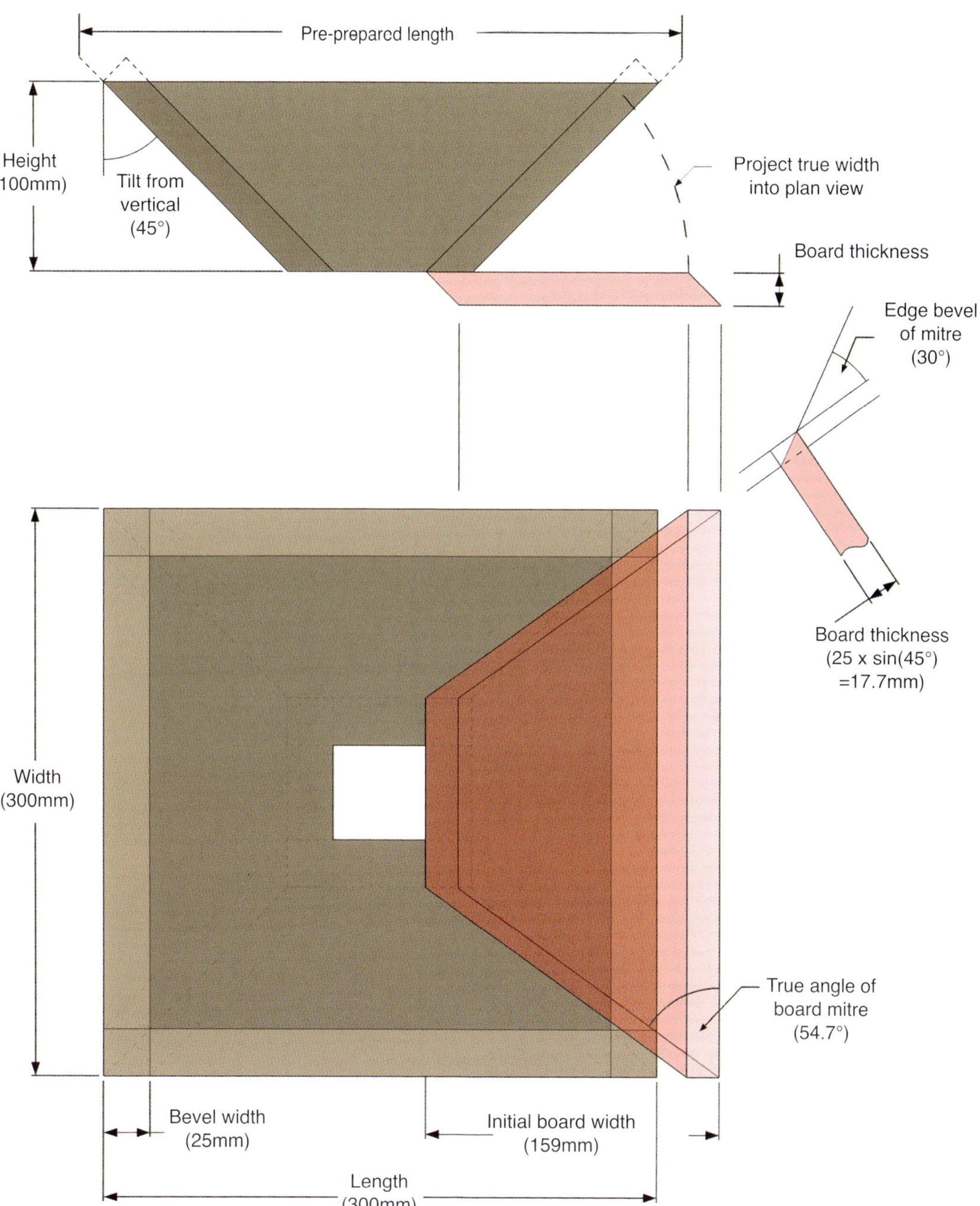


Using scale drawings to determine true lengths, the true mitre angle, and the edge bevel angle of a hopper.

be converted to the board width, edge bevel angle, and compound mitre angles required to construct it.

### 3D Modelling

A modern method of determining the component dimensions and true angles is to model the construction with one of the many 3D modelling applications now available.

True angles and dimensions can simply be measured within the model. However, this does require knowledge of how to use one of the applications.

## Initial Stock Preparation

However you determine the size of the initial components, they can be sawn from suitable stock, in the square, prepared to the width and thickness required.

A continuous grain match is impossible, since the board ends will be cut at an angle, so it can make sense to save waste and nest them when cutting from a long board.

It might seem sensible to work the edge bevels before the individual parts are cut from a board, however since the ends will need the mitre bevels shot, they will be easier to prepare

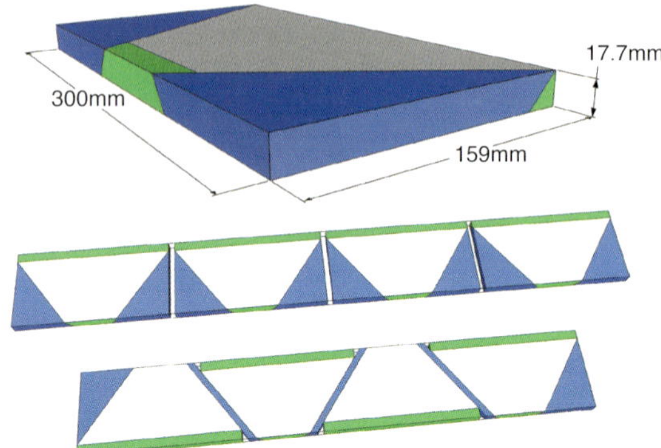

One side of the double-bevel hopper, within a squared blank, with the material to be removed clearly visible. It can make economic sense to nest the parts along a board. Here, both examples have the same saw kerf allowance between parts.

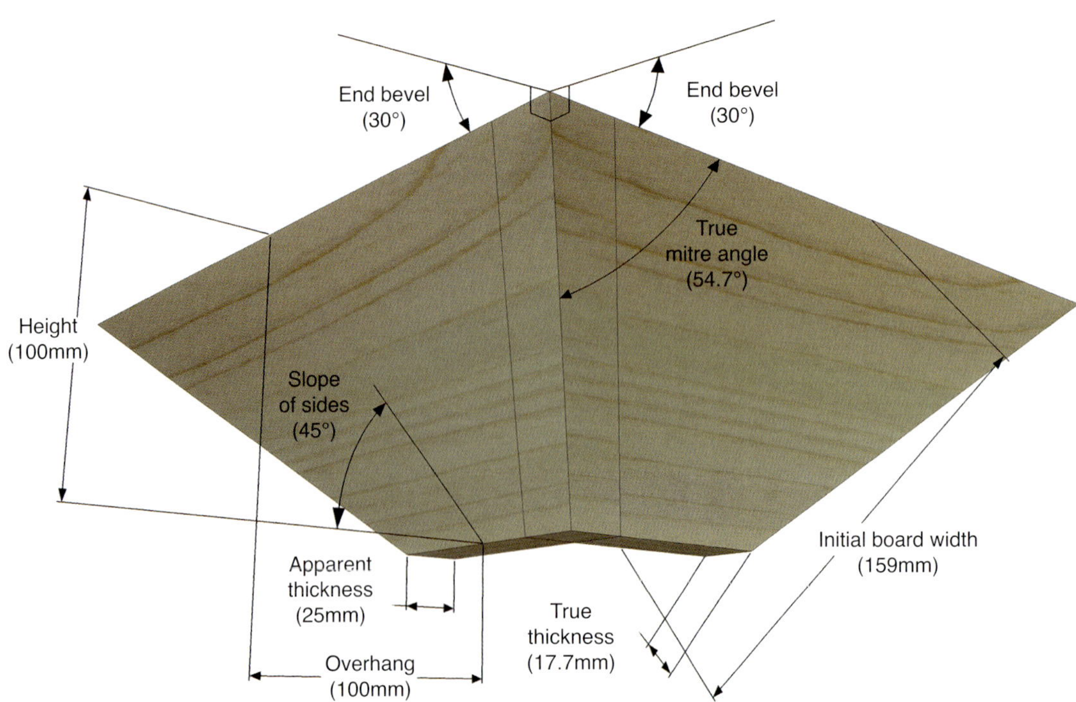

All the necessary measurements and angles can be taken directly from a 3D modelling package.

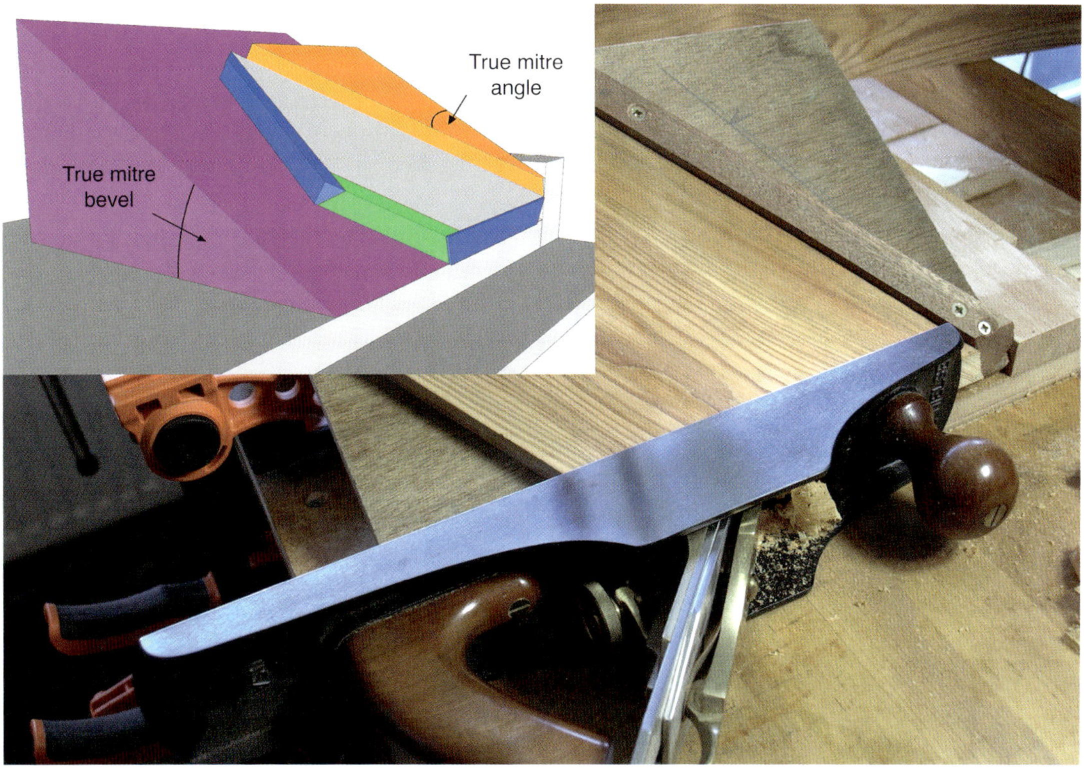

Shooting the bevelled mitre ends requires a pair of ramps or wedges (inset), or a custom-made hook, added to a standard shooting board.

The top and bottom edges are bevelled to slope the sides. Notice how this increases the apparent board thickness.

## ASYMMETRIC JOINTS

For symmetric joints, where the tilt and thickness are the same for both sides, only one set of compound angles needs to be found. In the case of asymmetric joints, both parts need to be considered, and the trigonometric equations are more complex; however, the direct and drawing projection, and the 3D modelling methods work just the same as described.

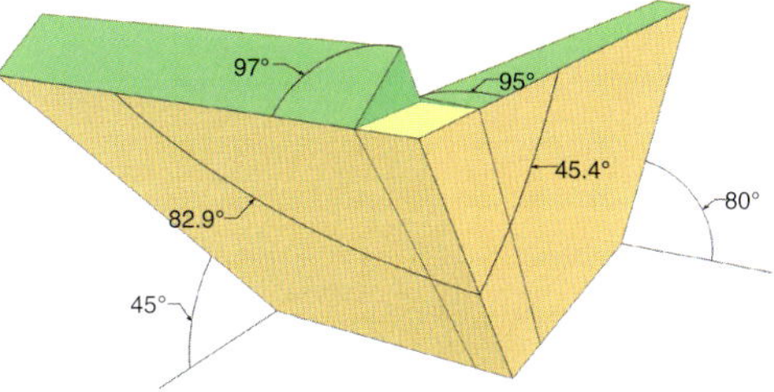


Asymmetric double-bevel dovetail angles found by 3D modelling.

if left square for the time being. So the parts are laid out along the board, allowing for the bevelled ends and a saw kerf between them, and then separated.

The compound mitred ends are first sawn close, then shot using an angled ramp and wedge, or alternative fixture, on a shooting board.

Bevelling each board's top and bottom edges readies them for dovetailing. The bevelled edges can significantly increase the observed thickness of the boards, and this should be taken into consideration during the design stage.

Marking the ends of the tails across the bevelled end of the tailboard. The blade of the bevel gauge must be kept tight to the end, and the stock brought up to the face side without twisting.

## Marking Out and Cutting

The face side of the tails are laid out as bevelled dovetails so they remain strong and look natural, but are then marked across the end grain using a bevel gauge. This is set to the edge bevel angle, and the blade flat must be held flat against the end of the board. The bevel gauge stock must be flat on all sides, as it will contact the face side of the tailboard along a corner edge, which needs to be straight and in a parallel plane to the blade.

The waste between the tails is clearly defined, before removal by sawing and paring. Because of the mitred and bevelled end, finding a comfortable position in which to clamp the board for sawing can be a challenge, and a pattern-maker's vise would be a huge help. I use either the front vise or a twin-screw vise, depending on the width of the board, and angle the saw to make the cuts.

To transfer the layout to the pinboard, I find it easiest to support it with its end in a horizontal plane, resting the tails on top. A card scraper held in the vise fractionally higher than the pinboard helps align the tailboard, while the location of the pin ends are knifed from the tails.

The pin sides are marked, parallel to the pinboard edges, using a pencil marking gauge.

With the tails marked out on two of the four boards used to make the double-bevel dovetail fruit bowl, I used a front vise to hold the boards while cutting the tails and pins. The saw has to be angled and tilted to follow the cut lines.

Transferring layout and marking the sides of the pins is more complicated than with regular dovetails. A card scraper clamped in front of the pinboard helps to keep the tailboard aligned as the layout is transferred with a scalpel (*left*). I ride the stock of a pencil gauge on the bevelled top of the pinboard while marking the pin sides (*right*).

With the pinboard held vertical in the front vise, the sockets can be sawn with the saw angled and tilted, but vertical (*left*). One joint is assembled to test the fit (*right*). Any stress should be relieved prior to gluing as clamping is awkward due to the sloped sides.

Next the pins are sawn. The cuts can be awkward to start on the angle, and a small notch or knife wall can be made if necessary. With all the cuts parallel to the edge of the pinboard I always clamp it vertically in the vise.

Once the sockets have been cleared the joint can be test fitted, and any adjustments made.

Clamping a double-bevel dovetail joint, or four in the case of a frame, is not easy when the boards are significantly sloped, and it is far easier to prepare the joint well enough so that it isn't under stress once assembled, and doesn't need clamping. However, shaped cauls can be temporarily glued to the sides to provide parallel clamping points.

**Pins First**

It is possible to prepare the double-bevel dovetail using a 'pins first' method. The same precautions during layout will apply due to the mitres and bevels as above.

A different double-bevel dovetail joint being prepared pins first. Transferring the pin layout to the tailboard.

Where mitres are the edge detail you are after, the mitre dovetail could be just the joint.

Example of the double-bevel dovetail, used to make a fruit bowl.

## THE MITRE DOVETAIL

The mitre dovetail is a variation of through or lapped dovetails, whose purpose is to present an alternative appearance to the joint's edge.

In both standard through or lapped dovetails the joint edge appears as a simple butt joint. Introducing a mitre adds a degree of refinement whilst maintaining much of the strength of the joint.

The mitre dovetail will often be found in dovetailed carcass construction, where the front of the carcass opening will be mitred.

The joint is prepared much the same as the underlying through or lapped dovetail, except that the end pin is halved on the diagonal to mate with material left outside the extreme tail of the tailboard. A single mitre can be created, or one at each end of the joint, usually determined by whether just one, or both ends are going to be on show.

### Initial Stock Preparation

In its simplest form the tailboard and pinboard will be prepared to the same thickness, and the whole end pin will eventually be sawn at 45 degrees. Where different thicknesses are used, the mitre can be prepared at an appropriate angle, joining the internal baseline to the external corner, or the mitre can be at 45 degrees and just cover a proportion of the thicker board.

Boards are prepared in the same way as for a through dovetail.

### Marking Out and Cutting

The thickness of each board is gauged on to the other, as for through dovetails, although the edges are omitted and receive an indicator as to the direction of the mitre.

A mitre gauge can be used when scribing the mitre between boards of equal thickness, or when a 45-degree mitre is wanted. Otherwise a

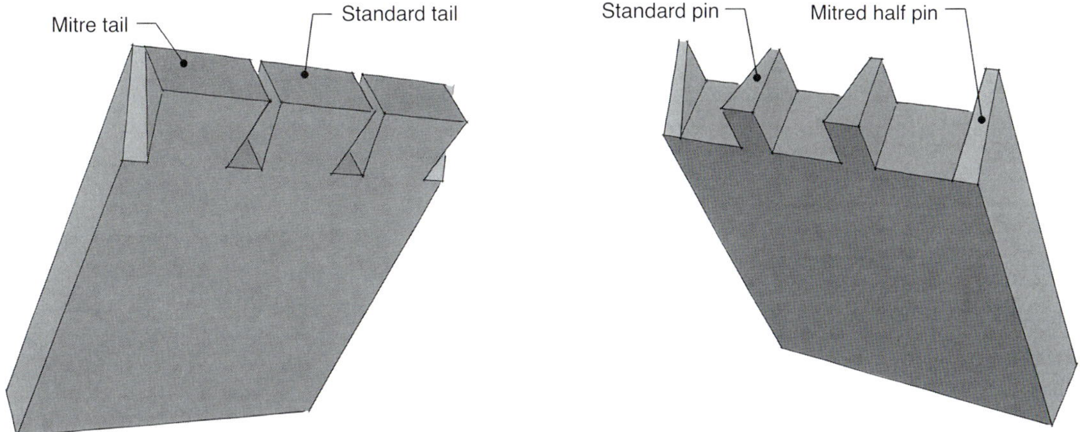


Through-mitre dovetail tail- and pinboards. Only the extreme tails and pins are any different from those of the through dovetail joint. The mitre need only be created on one side, especially if the other is never seen.

Tailboard and pinboard can be equal thicknesses and have a 45-degree mitre, or unequal thicknesses and have either a full mitre not at 45 degrees, or a 45-degree mitre plus a butt joint.

The tailboard has been gauged to the thickness of the pinboard, and a mitre line pencilled in connecting the inside corner to the outside corner (*left*). A bevel gauge was then used to knife in the bevel line, allowing a full mitre between boards of different thickness to be accurately scribed (*right*). For equal thickness joints, a standard mitre gauge could be used.

bevel gauge can be set and used for scribing the mitre with a marking knife.

Tails are marked out in the usual way, except that an additional allowance is made for the half-pins, which will be weakened by the mitre cut-out. Careful marking of the waste is critical to avoid sawing the mitre section off the extreme tail, or tails.

I suggest sawing the mitre-tail waste away first, before getting into the rhythm of sawing the rest of the tail sides. It is all too easy to cut through the whole of the extreme tail side, rather than just cutting the diagonal from the internal baseline to the external edge of the end.

Once the tailboard is prepared, use it as the template to transfer the layout to the pinboard. It is difficult to get right under the mitre tail with a knife, but do your best with a long pointed scalpel or similar. As with the tailboard, saw the mitre half-pins first before clearing the rest of the waste.

The two parts should assemble as a through dovetail, and as the tails reach the bottom of

Extra space is left for a wider mitre half-pin, while the rest of the tails are laid out as normal. The mitre tail is vulnerable to being sawn through, so it is carefully marked to show the waste (*left*), and I cut the mitre tails while I still remember that these are not regular ones. After that, the waste between tails can be removed as normal (*right*).

A pointed scalpel can reach most of the way under the mitre tail to transfer the layout accurately (*left*). Once sawn, the mitre should close tightly at the point where the tails bottom out in the sockets of the pinboard (*right*). If you leave the mitres a little heavy when initially cutting, you can pare them for the perfect fit.

## GREAT MITRES

Whether pins or tails are prepared first, it is reasonable to cut the mitres a little heavy to begin with, leaving room to pare them down for a tight fit. Remember a mitre that shows a gap should be avoided at all costs, since it is primarily there to improve the joint's appearance.

Completed joints should show the mitre precisely aligned to the corner. Any slight misalignment of the mitres external joint line can be corrected by planing one face more than the other.

Mitred and butt-jointed versions of secret dovetails, also known as double-lap dovetails, for times when you don't want to see the pins or tails.

the sockets, the edge mitre should close snugly. If the mitre appears to close early, or not well, check that the joint truly is at 90 degrees before making any adjustments. If the joint is less than 90 degrees the outside of the mitre will likely show a gap, or if more than 90 degrees the inside will.

### Pins First

In the 'pins first' method, the pins are marked and cut as usual, except that mitre half-pins are left wider. The layout is transferred to the tailboard, and finally the mitre marked and cut on the mitre pin or pins.

It is possible to prepare a mitre lapped dovetail, either mitring to the external corner or the lap line, and also mitred variants of many of the other dovetail joints shown in this book.

## THE SECRET (DOUBLE-LAP) DOVETAIL

Exposed dovetails are not necessarily desirable, usually depending on fashion, yet their mechanical properties often are. So-called secret dovetails (not to be confused with a secret mitre dovetail) are designed for these occasions, with the double-lap dovetail being the simplest. Three forms of this joint exist: those with a single extended lap on either the pin or tail board, and one with mitred, extended laps on both.

An extended lap on the pinboard (left), tailboard (centre), and mitred extended laps (right), are the three options when creating a secret dovetail. When disassembled, it's clear to see how the pins and tails are hidden.

Due to the presence of laps, which restrict access, it is most sensible for the pins to be cut first, and the tails marked from them.

For a demonstration I shall prepare a double-lap, with extended tail lap, dovetail, and then show the different finishing steps to a mitred double-lap dovetail joint.

### Initial Stock Preparation

The pinboard and tailboard are prepared square all round with their ends shot at 90 degrees, just as for a through dovetail. They don't need to be the same thickness or width, but they are in the demonstration joint I make here.

Unless just practising, lengths should be adjusted to account for the projecting lap when working from overall sizes. For example, where the projecting lap is on the pinboard, the length of the tailboard will be reduced by the thickness of the lap.

## Marking Out and Cutting

First set a marking gauge to the thickness of the pinboard, and gauge in the baseline for the tails on the inside surface of the tailboard.

A lap of approximately 3mm (1/8in) is suitable for most domestic furniture, and is marked in on both pinboard and tailboard, from their front surfaces.

Just for the tailboard, carry on the lap marking, referenced now from the end of the board so as to enclose an area of waste to be removed to leave a rebate in the end grain.

Set a marking gauge to the thickness of the rebate, which will be the length of the pins, and gauge in the baseline for the pinboard on its inside face.

Once the pins have been laid out and cut, in the same way as for the lapped dovetail, the pinboard is used to transfer the layout

The rebate that will be cut to leave the extension to the lap on the tailboard (*left*), and the lap extension on the tailboard that will cover the end of the pinboard lap (*right*).

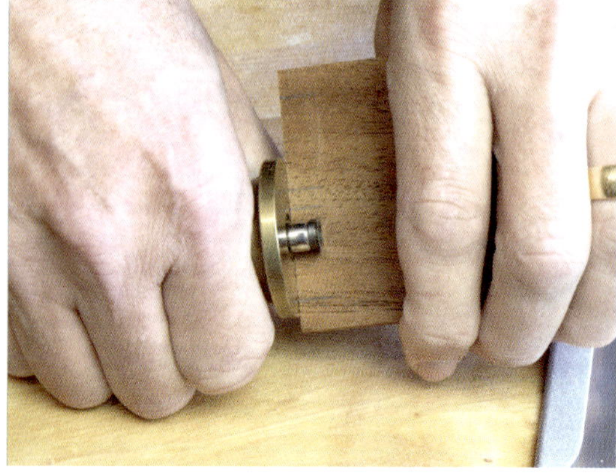

The distance to the lap extension across the tailboard end will be how far the pins need to insert in the tails (*left*). Gauge the inside face of the pinboard with a baseline to which the sockets between pins will be cut (*right*).

to the tailboard. The lap extension is used as the reference against which the outside of the pinboard is aligned for the transfer, after which the waste to be cleared from the tailboard is clearly marked.

The tails should now be cut, starting by sawing on a diagonal and avoiding cutting into the extended lap. The waste is mainly removed by chopping, although in large joints there may be a benefit in boring some of the waste with a drill first. The tails are completed, and any final fit achieved with careful paring.

With the pinboard aligned to the lap extension, the layout is transferred for the tails (*left*). The completed pinboard, and the tailboard marked ready to cut the lapped tails (*right*).

Only a limited amount of sawing can be used to cut the tails due to the extended lap (*left*), and most of the waste will be chopped and pared to complete the tailboard ready for assembly (*right*).

## A MITRED DOUBLE LAP

A gauge is used to mark baselines for the pins and tails on the inside faces of their respective boards.

The lap thickness is marked on the inside and edges of the ends of both pinboard and tailboard, and this extended lap waste is removed.

The pins are laid out, cut, and the layout transferred to the tailboard. Tails are cut and fitted as before, and the two parts assembled as far as possible.

The extended laps interfere, preventing the joint from fully closing. The mitres are marked in on both laps with a mitre gauge, before the joint is taken apart and the mitres worked to a snug fit using a mitre guide block and paring chisel.

Having prepared both pinboard and tailboard with extended laps, a mitre square is used to mark in the mitre cuts needed to complete a mitred double-lap dovetail.

Paring the mitre joint for the mitred double-lap dovetail, with the help of a shop-made mitre guide block.

## THE SECRET MITRE (FULL BLIND) DOVETAIL

The apex of secret dovetail joints is the secret mitre, or full blind dovetail. In terms of preparation it is not much more difficult than the mitred double-lap dovetail described above, however in my opinion the appearance of the full mitre on the edges is aesthetically far more superior.

The pinnacle of secret dovetail joints, the secret mitre dovetail, or full blind dovetail. This particular joint is from a contemporary writing slope, and is made in East Indian rosewood.

### Initial Stock Preparation

The initial stock preparation is the same as for through dovetails or mitre dovetails. Equal thicknesses will result in true 45-degree mitres, which definitely look best.

### Marking Out and Cutting

Looking at the prepared joint pieces, it should be recognised that this joint is identical to the mitred double-lap dovetail in all but the appearance of the edges, which are prepared as for the mitre dovetail.

Consequently the ends of both pinboard and tailboard can be prepared with identical rebates, leaving lips that will be mitred for the outside corner of the joint.

The pinboard is marked out using a flat dovetail guide and try-square, and the end pins are marked with a full mitre extending to the outside corner, similar to the mitre dovetail. The pins are cut making sure to protect the outside edge of the board, which closes the mitre and will be very visible.

The tailboard is now marked directly from the pinboard, using an awl or pointed knife, and the extreme edges marked with a mitre to the outside corners.

When cutting the tails, the outside edge of the board should be protected, and the edge waste of the outside tails sawn against the mitre line.

The edge mitres are pared close to the line and to the outside corner, before paring or planing the length of the corner mitre, using a

Sawing the pins as much as possible, while avoiding damage to the outside of what will be the corner mitre.

The prepared pieces of a secret mitre dovetail, very similar to the mitred double-lap dovetail, except for the two short mitred edges.

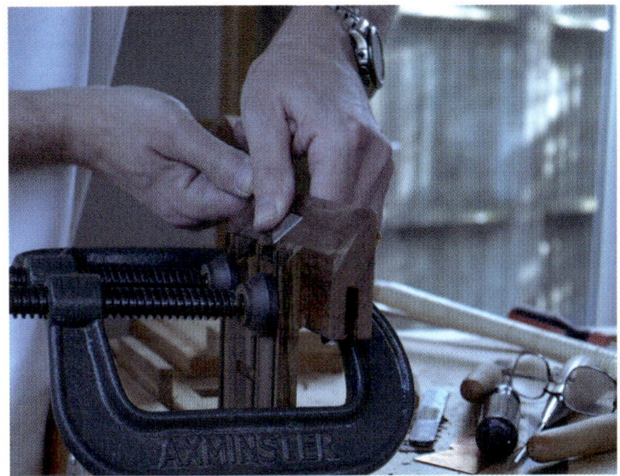


Paring the corner mitre on the tailboard, with the mitre guide block clamped to the board for guidance.

The rebate cut, and the pin layout marked for a secret mitre dovetail. Notice the grooves and non-uniform pin layout that I used when making my writing slope.

There is no clue to the existence of dovetail joints in my writing slope, thanks to the secret mitre dovetail.

mitre guide block. In order for the entire mitre to close tightly, the joint should be fitted and tried as the mitre joint is finally pared towards its lines. The lines are truly no more than a guide, and achieving a well fitted joint with a tight mitre is more important than hitting all the lines exactly.

If the mitres are prepared to a tight fit through their thickness, then the finished joint can be smoothed, eased, shaped or sanded without risk of the mitre opening up.

## THE ART DECO DOVETAIL

This is the first of a few decorative dovetail joints that I designed myself, and it was inspired by the Art Deco period. Only the standard tails are full depth, with the inlaid background just a quarter or so, which maintains a good degree of structural strength.

### Initial Stock Preparation

Pinboard and tailboard should be prepared squared all round, with squared ends, just as for a standard through or lapped dovetail. The secondary wood that creates the background contrast on the pinboard end should have the end grain shot square to at least one wide face, and preferably large enough to yield the inlay in a single slice.

### Marking Out and Cutting

The design calls for a single slope angle for both the true lapped tails and the contrast inlay. The proportions should be chosen to provide both a strong and aesthetically pleasing joint. Multiple groupings should be used for wide joints, and different proportions can be used for extra decoration.

The contrast inlay should be marked out on the end grain of the donor board, and a slice cut from it. This end-grain piece will be quite fragile until the whole joint is glued, and you could apply some low viscosity CA glue to it, to give it a little more resilience.

Using a craft knife or scalpel and a sharp chisel, cut away the excess material from the slice to leave the inlay. This sounds easier than it is, as the end grain is prone to crack beyond the point being cut. Use this property to your advantage where you can, and where you can't, take very small bites at a time. The trickiest spot is working into corners, and if the inlay ends up being in two or three pieces, this is not a problem as it can be reassembled with glue.

Now use the inlay as a template for marking the cavity that it will fill in the pinboard. Mark as tight to the inlay as possible to avoid any gaps, and provide plenty of support when the inlay is glued in. Deepen the knifed layout lines to 2mm (3/32in), and then carefully pare away the waste to the bottom to create a pocket.

The Art Deco period was the inspiration behind my Art Deco dovetail.

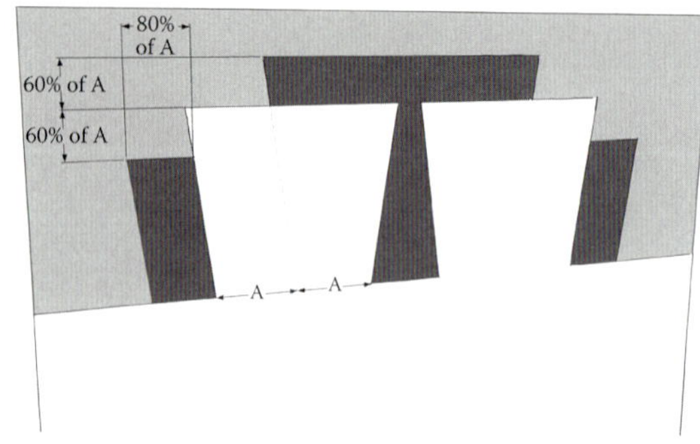


These proportions I find work well, but are not strict. The slope of the tails should match the materials being used, and each twin dovetail grouping should be repeated as required across wide joints.

After drawing out the contrast inlay a 2mm (3/32in) slice is cut from the donor board (*left*). The shape of the inlay is carefully revealed by cutting away the excess material (*right*). The short grain may break during these stages, but it can be reassembled when gluing in.

A knife is used to transfer the inlay shape to the pinboard, ready for a pocket to be excavated (*left*). This pocket is simply pared down to depth between the knifed walls (*right*).

With the tail layout transferred to the pinboard the sides of the sockets can be sawn (*left*), and a sharp chisel used to complete the preparation of the pins without dislodging the small inlays (*right*).

Glue the inlay into the pinboard socket, and leave to cure properly before flushing it to the surface with a block plane. A CA glue would be the best option if you previously used it to strengthen the inlay slice.

After preparing the tails in the usual way, the tailboard is used to mark in for the pins on top of the inlaid pinboard. Then saw the sides of the sockets as you would a lapped dovetail, making sure not to cut too far into the inlay.

Chop out the waste and pare to a good fit. Remember the inlay is only really held by the end-grain to end-grain glue joint, and may break away if it is struck directly. Glue and assemble the joint in the same way as a normal lapped dovetail, and when cured, carefully flush the tailboard with the pinboard.

Clearly the same technique can be used to produce a multitude of decorated dovetail joints – and why stop at just one contrast wood, when there are so many to choose from?

## CURVED DOVETAILS

Designs incorporating curved dovetails appear quite limited, however the techniques for preparing them all are quite simple, once basic dovetailing is mastered. Here I shall present two examples, whose design I initially experimented with in a simple 3D modelling package. They are the lapped dovetail to a cove, and a through dovetail to an arc.

### Initial Stock Preparation

Although it is generally easiest to start with squared all round components, extreme curves will lead to a lot of waste removal from a pinboard after the joint is prepared. As a minimum, it makes sense to prepare pinboards with a flat inside face and squared edges and ends. Tailboards should have parallel inside and outside faces, and squared edges.

### Marking Out and Cutting

**Lapped Dovetail to a Cove**

The external and internal curves of the lap are scribed on the end of the pinboard with sharp

Two examples of curved dovetails, a through dovetailed arc, and a lapped dovetail cove. Preliminary sketches can be drawn freehand or in 3D modelling software, to test the design before committing to wood.

A hand screw clamped to the pinboard extends the end surface enough to swing the desired arcs for the front face and lap line (*left*). With the spring dividers unchanged, the profile for the end of the tailboard is scribed, ensuring a good match (*right*).

spring dividers. The centre point for these arcs can be positioned outside the pinboard end by clamping on an extension to the board, expanding the surface plane.

The matching arc for the end of the tailboard can be scribed on to it using a similar arrangement. Doing these arcs one after the other allows the spring dividers setting to be maintained throughout.

After the baseline for the tails is added, they can be laid out. The slope should be consistent and suitable for the type of wood being used, as previously covered, but the neck size and spacing should be chosen for the best aesthetic. Testing the layout directly on the pinboard gives me a good idea of what the finished joint will look like.

The other end of the pinboard has been used to test the layout, before committing it to the tailboard.

Prepare the curve on the tailboard by sawing and then filing to the scribed line, then saw the tails and chop out the waste. The completed tailboard is then used as the template to transfer the layout for the pins. With such long tails, a 'pins first' approach would be impossible here.

The pins are sawn, chopped and pared as for standard lapped dovetails, with extra care as the curve is approached. Skew chisels, carving gouges and scalpels can all aid in cleaning out the awkward sockets. Focus on fitting to the curve well, as any gaps will be hard to disguise in figured end grain.

Once all the joinery is completed on the pinboard, the waste outside the curve can be removed. This will often be easier before the joint is assembled, but do consider how the assembled joint can be planed flush and held whilst doing so.

### Through Dovetail to an Arc

In this example a flat tailboard joins to a pinboard with an arc profile. Both outside and inside faces of the pinboard are concentric arcs, although it is not necessary to shape either.

The baseline for the tails should be a concentric arc, with the partial exception of the outside shoulders, where a squared baseline prevents a fragile, feathered half-pin.

The tailboard end should be prepared square initially and the tails set out and marked as

The tailboard is used as a template to transfer the layout for the pins (*left*). Clearing out the pinboard sockets is the same as for standard lapped dovetails, however the curved lap line presents a challenge, often requiring some very narrow chisels and sharp knives (*right*)

When dovetailing to an arc, the tails are spaced as normal, but are extended down to the arc of the baseline. They should be sized wide enough so that the necks are not too small.

usual, except that the tail sides extend down to the arc baseline. Take care that the necks of the outside tails don't end up too narrow. This would make them weak and the mating sockets would be harder to clean out.

Once the tails have been cut, they can be used to transfer the layout to the pinboard. This is easier to do if the pinboard is first prepared in the square, and its arc profile is shaped later on. If the pinboard profile has already been prepared, ensuring that the alignment of the tailboard to the pinboard is square takes more care.

The waste around the pins, having been clearly marked, should be removed, and once

When transferring the layout from the tailboard, it is easier for alignment if the pinboard has not yet been shaped (*left*). A fretsaw is used to remove the waste between pins and also to undercut the waste behind the baseline (*right*).

A shallow gouge helps to pare the back of the pins to the arc (left). After shaping the rear of the pinboard before assembly, the ends of the tails and the front of the pinboard are shaped after the joint has been glued.

again I find this is easier to do before shaping the profile.

After the joint is well fitted, the inside of the pinboard can be shaped, as this will be very difficult after the joint is finally assembled. The outside profile of the pinboard can also be shaped, however I prefer to do this if possible after the joint is assembled, as the ends of the tails can be shaped at the same time. Clamping sacrificial pieces to the tailboard can help prevent splintering during the shaping process.

## THE DOUBLE DOVETAIL

Much seen in the marketing of jigs used with power routers, the double dovetail joint can be quite easily prepared with hand tools, although joints do take about twice as long as their equivalent standard through dovetails.

### Initial Stock Preparation

Pinboard and tailboard should be prepared in the primary wood, squared all around, with squared ends, just as for a standard through or lapped dovetail. A third board should be

The double dovetail joint is well named as it takes double the effort to prepare it compared to a standard through dovetail.

### BREAKING DOWN THE DOUBLE DOVETAIL

As its name suggests, in this joint there are two dovetail joints in one: firstly a through dovetail with a slight difference, where the contrast wood is the tailboard and the pins have a rear rebate; followed by a second through dovetail, where the tails have a rear rebate and the pins are cut into the contrast wood. This may sound confusing, but the illustration should make things clear.

The rear rebates allow for the contrast highlighting to appear at the baselines of the pins and tails externally, while covering it up internally. If the rebates are left out, then a square section of contrast runs down the inside of the joint.

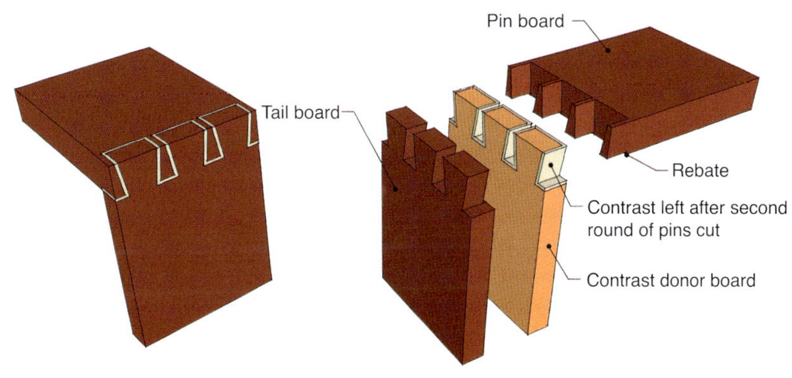


An assembled double dovetail and its exploded view, also showing the whole donor contrast board with what remains and what is removed.

prepared similarly, but only needs to be long enough to hold safely while cutting a set of tails. It should be the same thickness as the actual tailboard.

## Marking Out and Cutting

The thickness of the tailboard is gauged round the pinboard, and the thickness of the pinboard is gauged round both the tailboard and the contrast board. Then a foreshortened baseline is gauged on the contrast board, and the same distance gauged from the face of the pinboard across its end grain and along its edges to its own baseline. This foreshortening is equal to the thickness that the contrast highlighting is desired to be, and something in the order of one sixth to one eighth of the tailboard thickness.

Tails are marked out on the contrast board, together with what will be the pins for the actual tailboard to fit to later on. Although it is usual to allow the same contrast thickness between tails and pins as for the contrast baselines, it isn't strictly necessary.

The tails on the contrast board are sawn and then pared clean and square. Once

An additional, foreshortened baseline on the contrast board shows where the tails are cut to. The far baseline will be where the donor board is cut off, leaving a contrast line.

The contrast board marked out with the tails that will be cut initially, removing the designated waste, and the layout of pins to be cut later on.

The contrast tails are the template for transferring the layout to the pinboard (*left*). The pins have been sawn, and the backs of them are about to be rebated to allow for the contrast highlight (*right*).

A foreshortened baseline for the pinboard is gauged in, leaving the contrast line at the rear of the sockets (*left*). A backing board is used to protect the contrast as the pins are sawn and the sockets cleaned up (*right*).

Aligning the boards in a hand screw while the final tail layout is transferred from the contrast pins (*left*). The tail waste is clearly defined, along with the rebate that will cover the contrast up on the inside of the joint (*right*).

completed, they are used to transfer the layout to the pinboard.

The pins and the rebate for the contrast are then cut, and any adjustments made for a snug fit.

The contrast tails are glued into the pinboard and left to cure, after which the excess contrast board is sawn off.

Before the final pins can be cut, the foreshortened baseline is marked in, to leave the contrast at the back of the sockets.

Now the pins are prepared for the second time, taking precautions to preserve the recently

The completed joint has been fitted and is ready to assemble with glue.

glued contrast, ready to be used to transfer the layout for the tails to the tailboard.

The tailboard must be rebated by the contrast thickness, so this rebate is marked in and the waste for it and the tails defined.

Once the rebate and tails are prepared and the joint fitted, it is ready to glue.

## THE HOUNDSTOOTH DOVETAIL

Another popular decorative dovetail is the houndstooth, or long and short tails dovetail. Wider than usual tails are divided up by short pins, which add some strength back as well as providing visual interest. The length of the short pins is up to the designer, but something between a half and two thirds of that of the regular pins is normal.

A standard houndstooth dovetail joint, with a single small pin in the outside centre of each tail.

There are many design variations possible, some including elements from other dovetail forms.

### Initial Stock Preparation

Pinboard and tailboard should be prepared squared all round, with squared ends, just as for a standard through or lapped dovetail. To accommodate the different sized pins, the pinboard is kept on the thicker side.

### Marking Out and Cutting

The pinboard and tailboard thicknesses are gauged round each other, as for through dovetails. The gauge is then set to the short pin length, which is gauged across the pinboard end, referenced from the outside, and also across the faces of the tailboard end, to give the short-tail baselines.

Assuming a 'tails first' approach, the tailboard is first divided up into wide tails, after which these tails are subdivided into the distinctive narrower tails.

The tails are cut in the normal way, paying particular attention to the depth of each saw cut, and the baseline it should reach to avoid mistakes. The completed tailboard is used to transfer the layout to the pinboard.

The pinboard waste should be clearly marked, with the small pins that need to be preserved identified. The pin sides are sawn and the waste removed. Sawing the waste across the bottom as much as possible, with a fretsaw or

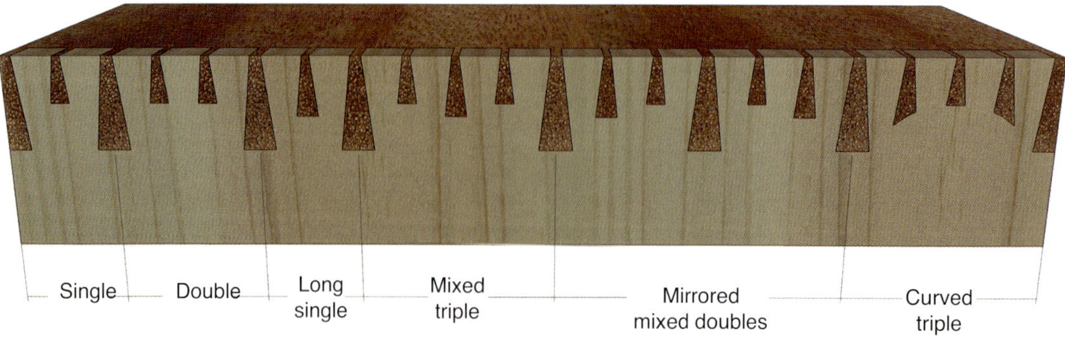


There are many possible variations on the houndstooth dovetail, of which these are just a few. (The names are my own, as no published source could be found.)

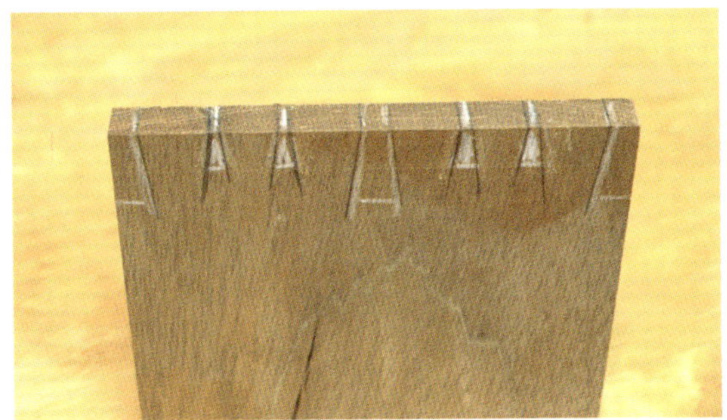

The primary tails are laid out first in the normal way, then treated individually almost as separate tailboards, where the secondary tails are marked in and the waste material defined.

The pinboard and tailboard after removing all the marked waste and ready for gluing.

Transferring the houndstooth layout from the tailboard to the pinboard. In most cases the small pins will have narrow necks and it will require a fine-bladed knife such as a scalpel to reach into these properly.

The completed joint with double short pins in each main tail.

When sawing the baseline of the socket waste, start by leaving the waste behind the short pins. This provides more freedom to undercut the remaining waste with the saw angled first one way and then the other.

similar, prevents the need to chop across the grain. Paring cuts are used to level the sockets to the baseline. Where the grain allows, vertical paring of the waste behind the short pins is a quick option.

Final fit, gluing up and planing smooth is just like that for a standard through dovetail.

## THE SHADOW DOVETAIL

Like the double dovetail, shadow dovetails are designed for aesthetic purposes. The effect can be prepared with thin end-grain inlays, as the Art Deco dovetail shown earlier, but I favour working them in face grain, which I feel is easier and more resilient.

Different designs and layouts are possible, all with the intention of suggesting the tails are not flush with the pinboard and are casting shadows.

## Initial Stock Preparation

Prepare a pinboard and tailboard as for a standard lapped dovetail, and a second, usually thinner, tailboard in a darker wood.

A simple example of shadow dovetails, showing how the technique can emphasise the dovetails in similar toned wood joints.

## Marking Out and Cutting

The second tailboard is marked out for tails in the usual way, except that an extra allowance is added to the half-pin spacing equal to the thickness of the desired shadow line. Then the pinboard and the second tailboard are lap dovetailed, and the tails cut off at the baseline.

The pinboard is next marked out, but with the sockets shifted to the opposite direction by the thickness of the desired shadow line, and with the length of the tails shortened by the same amount. This time the baseline is matched to the thickness of the tailboard that will remain.

Once the sockets have been cleaned out, the pinboard is used to transfer the layout to the tailboard in the usual way, and the tails cut and fitted.

Using the same technique, but with a lighter wood instead of a darker wood, the illusion of highlights can be achieved.

Well fitted, and assuming a good glue bond between the tail side and its shadow, the strength of these joints should be comparable

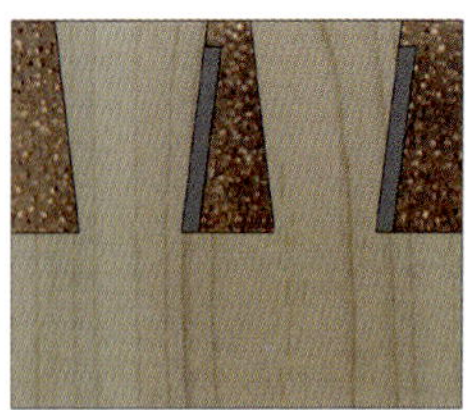

Examples of shadow dovetails. Through and lapped dovetails, suggesting lighting from the lower left, and a wide, lapped dovetail suggesting lighting from a central position in front of the tailboard.

First prepare a lapped dovetail with the tails in a darker colour, and cut off the tailboard at the baseline.

The final true sockets are prepared, offset from the contrasting shadow tails that were previously glued in place, leaving the shadow lines.

Completed, the illusion can be quite effective, and worth the extra effort.

My swallowtail joint is just a new variation on dovetails. Interestingly dovetail joints are known as swallowtail joints in parts of Europe.

with standard dovetails having tails of the same length as those on the final tailboard.

## THE SWALLOWTAIL DOVETAIL

Having found no other reference to this joint, I decided to call it a swallowtail joint. I feel it bears enough resemblance to a dovetail joint in appearance, preparation and function, that it should be classed as one. I include its preparation here, both in the through and lapped versions.

### Initial Stock Preparation

Prepare tail- and pinboards square and true, and shoot the ends square, in the normal fashion for through and lapped dovetails.

Baselines are gauged on the tailboards for the tail length, according to whether the joint will be through or lapped. Where lapped, the tail length is also gauged on the end of the pinboard.

The tails are spaced off equally with spring dividers, and the outside of the tails are pencilled in using an 8:1 dovetail marking gauge.

To create the swallowtail profile, the diagonals are drawn on the plain tails and the outside triangle of the four created is set for removal.

The thickness of the tailboards is scribed across the faces of the pinboards, defining the baseline for the sockets.

Shooting the ends of the boards square in preparation for marking out the swallowtail joints.

Marking in the diagonals of plain tails in order to define the waste to be removed at the end of the tail. Using the diagonals to do this makes cutting the pins an easier task.

## Marking Out and Cutting

Saw the tails in the normal way, and saw free the waste triangle at the end of them all.

Tailboards are used to transfer the shape of the tails on to the ends of the pinboards in the usual way, but also including the cut-out in the tails.

When sawing the pin sides and the waste triangle, the same vertical kerf is used, keeping the cuts aligned and crisp. By using the diagonals to mark the triangle of waste, sawing the pins is made as easy as possible.

Chop out the waste on the pinboard in two stages: first, down to the tip of the triangle, and then with a thinner chisel either side of it.

The waste in the tips of the lapped swallowtail pins can be cleaned out using a scalpel, or a bevel cut on the back of the corresponding tail corner to avoid it.

Sawing the triangles from the ends of the tails, and clearing the rest of the waste, while preparing the tailboards.

The tail notches should be transferred with the rest of the tail layout to the pinboard end.

Using the same saw kerf to start the cut for the triangle pin, as used to cut the socket sides.

Carefully chopping the waste from the sockets to retain the central triangle that fits in the tail notch. In lapped swallowtails, the rear corners of the sockets are very difficult to clean out.

Completed through and lapped swallowtail dovetail joints.

## THE MECHANICS OF WOODEN DOVETAILS: PART 2

### Slope Angle versus Strength

Sufficient force will pull a dovetail joint apart, but how does the slope angle affect this failure?

Intuitively, the lower the slope angle, the smaller the flare of a tail, and the less compression needed to allow it to pass through the gap between pins. However, years of evolution hasn't resulted in high slope angles to give greater joint strength. The reason for this is that the extremes of tails are short grain, and liable to fail, by shearing when stressed, so decreasing the amount of compression required for total joint failure. It is the balance between the forces compressing the tail, and acting to shear off the tail flares, or sections thereof, that results in the strongest mechanical joint.

To complicate matters, different woods have different compression and shearing figures, which would result in a broad range of theoretically ideal slope angles for strength. Also, the shear strength initially increases as the wood is compressed.

As a very general rule, softwood compresses more easily and will perform better with a higher slope angle (1:4 to 1:5), whereas hardwood will work well with a modest slope angle (1:6 to 1:8), and dense exotics, which barely compress under normal loads, will happily cope with a low slope angle (1:9). In practice, more consideration tends to be given to joint aesthetics or machining options.

Glue is covered in The Mechanics of Wooden Dovetails: Part 3, at the end of the next chapter.

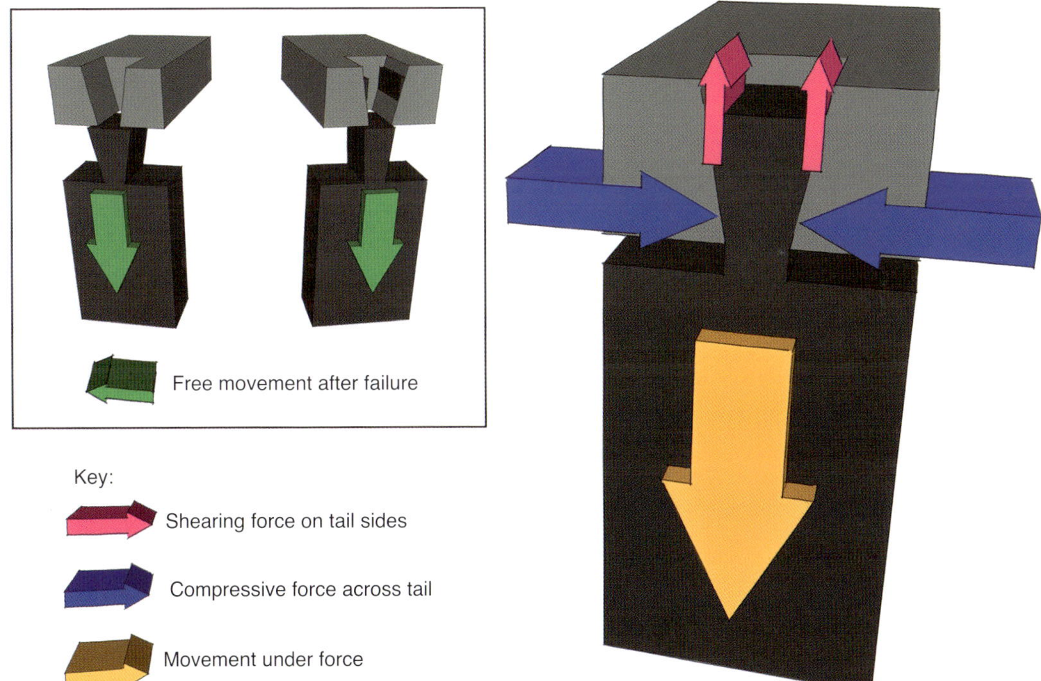


Unglued joint under tension, and failure (inset) where the whole tail is pulled through, and a partial tail pulled through after the sides shear.

CHAPTER 5

# MISCELLANEOUS JOINTS

Dovetails appear in many different places, and in many different designs. The corner joints in the previous chapter probably account for the vast majority of dovetails seen in finished furniture and cabinets, however behind the scenes and in less obvious places, the functional ability of dovetails sees them used extensively.

This chapter will show the preparation of the less obvious dovetail joinery to be found in the world around us, joinery that we don't often see as mere users of the items they are employed in. In addition it will show the preparation of some joints commonly known as dovetails, but whose appearance is either unlike the common notion of a dovetail, or which defy logic at first sight but are functionally valuable.

Tying the top of a post and side rail into each other and into a front rail, the carcass dovetail joint can be found in both traditional and good quality contemporary furniture.

## THE CARCASS/ LEG AND RAIL DOVETAIL

Whether tying the sides of a post and frame carcass or a solid panel carcass into a top bearer rail, the carcass dovetail joint can be widely found in cheap utility furniture from the post-war period, as well as in good quality contemporary furniture. Sound joints such as these are just part of stiffening up carcasses, essential in maintaining the free functioning of drawers and doors.

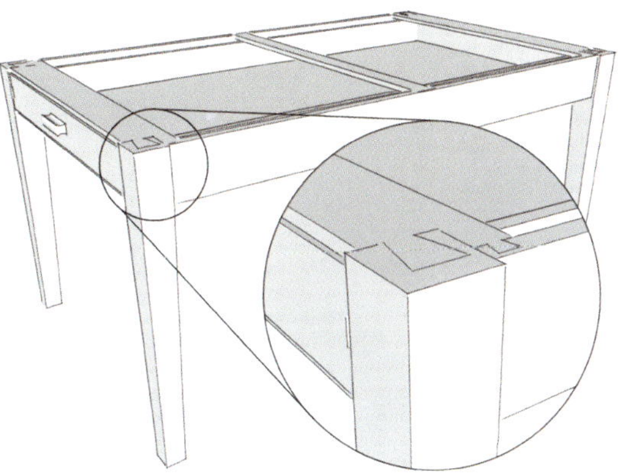

The carcass dovetail in use holding the upper drawer rail to the side rail and leg.

Some miscellaneous dovetail joints covered in Chapter 5.

Farmhouse and kitchen tables in solid wood will sometimes incorporate carcass dovetails to help frame wide drawer openings in rails, keeping their legs well tied into the frame.

There are variations depending on the design and construction, but understanding the preparation of the example shown in the illustration should enable you to adapt the method to suit the circumstances.

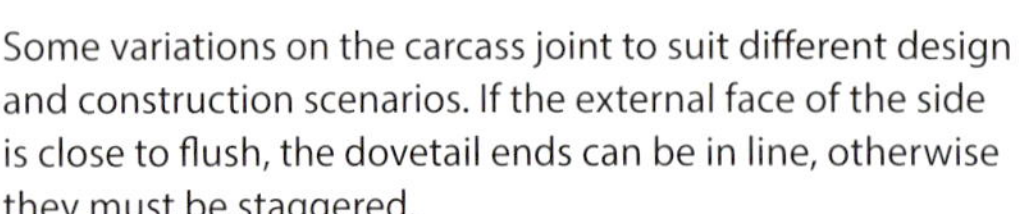

Some variations on the carcass joint to suit different design and construction scenarios. If the external face of the side is close to flush, the dovetail ends can be in line, otherwise they must be staggered.

If furniture making is your intended vocation, this is a joint you should get to know well.

## Initial Stock Preparation

Parts are all prepared square and true, and where a post is involved, this is first joined to the panel or rail making up the side. This will normally involve a tenon, and to accommodate the top bearer rail later on, this tenon should be sufficiently haunched, such that the main tenon lies below the dovetail of the top bearer rail.

## Marking Out and Cutting

Set the top bearer rail in position on top of the post, and mark in the tail baselines from the side rail and post, together with the position of the back of the post. Knife the baselines round to the top of the bearer rail to ensure crisp shoulder cuts.

### TOP BEARER LENGTH

The top bearer rail length is determined by setting the sides in place and measuring the total width across the posts, then deducting one third of the post width so that the dovetails will reach across five-sixths of each post.

These fractions are a guide, and some leeway is acceptable. In fact it simplifies matters if the ends of both dovetails can be in line with each other, although the post dovetail should not be overly shortened to achieve this.

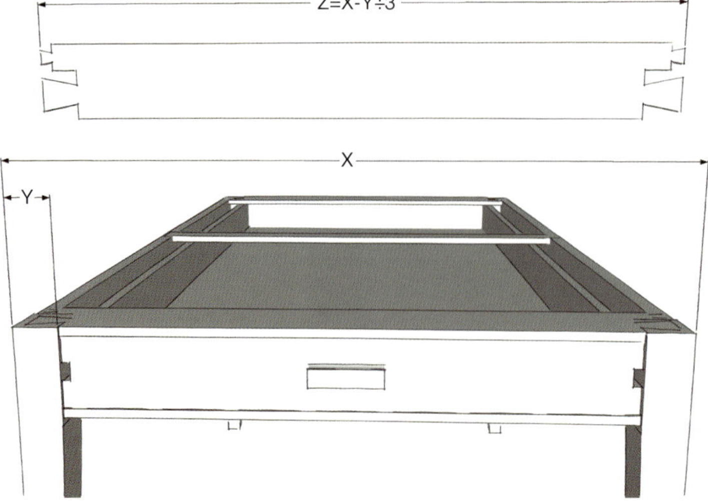


Determining the length of the top bearer rail, by measuring the full width and the post width, and doing a simple calculation.

Direct method of marking the baseline for the dovetail into the side rail. A marking gauge could be set to do the same task.

Spacing the tails so they avoid the haunch between the side rail and post.

Direct method of marking the baseline for the dovetail into the side rail. A marking gauge could be set to do the same task.

A one-in-five dovetail marking gauge helps lay out the tails down to the baselines.

Also mark in a line for the back of the sockets on the post and side rail, from the end of the top bearer rail, and the spacing for the tails on the end of the top bearer rail.

Mark in the dovetail sides, down to the baselines, and saw them.

Remove the waste and use the tails to transfer the layout to the top of the post and side rail.

Saw and pare the sockets, in the same way as for lapped dovetails.

A more rigorous method of marking out can be adopted using a marking gauge to define the lengths of tails, scribe baselines, and gauge

Once cut, the tails are used to directly mark out the positions for the sockets in the post and rail.

Cleaning out the post socket after sawing the sides as much as possible. The same procedure as cutting sockets for lapped dovetails is used.

The completed carcass dovetail. The tails ended on the same line in this example, but if the side rail is inset more, its tail would be held back appropriately.

the notch round the post; however, the direct method given here has always produced exceptionally well fitted joints.

## THE DOVETAIL BRIDLE

The common 'T' bridle joint is most notably used to connect a leg, or legs, to the middle of a continuous rail. With glue, this provides an excellent attachment. However, by adding dovetail details, an extra level of mechanical capture can be achieved. The dovetail bridle joint does just that.

The joint is simplest to prepare with parallel dovetails, however when fitted well it can be a struggle to assemble when glue is applied, and so a taper is often added to the dovetails. This tapered joint is designed to tighten up as the parts come together, and as well as easing glued assemblies, it can be a most useful knock-down joint when used dry.

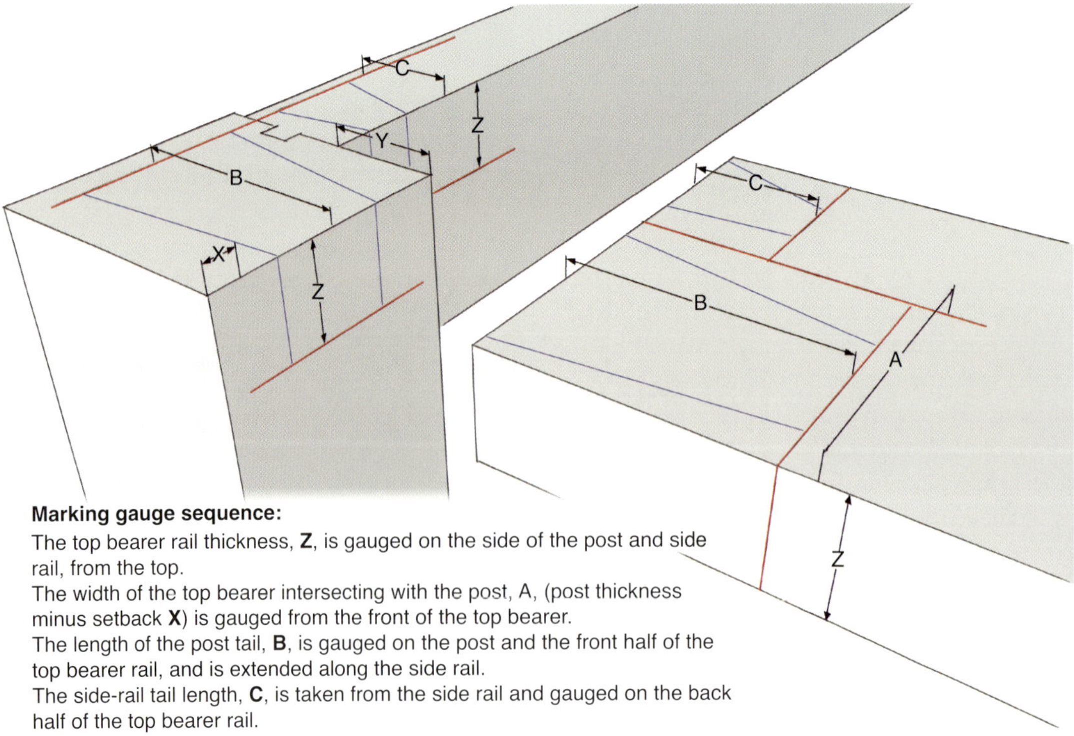

**Marking gauge sequence:**

The top bearer rail thickness, **Z**, is gauged on the side of the post and side rail, from the top.
The width of the top bearer intersecting with the post, A, (post thickness minus setback **X**) is gauged from the front of the top bearer.
The length of the post tail, **B**, is gauged on the post and the front half of the top bearer rail, and is extended along the side rail.
The side-rail tail length, **C**, is taken from the side rail and gauged on the back half of the top bearer rail.

A marking gauge method for laying out the foundations of a carcass dovetail joint.

The dovetail bridle joint, a dovetail version of the common bridle joint.

Initial marking out is very similar to that of a common bridle joint, except that the rail is only marked on its bottom edge.

Legs joining a continuous rail, using dovetail bridle joints. When parts are the same thickness the dovetail joint is visible, but if the leg is sufficiently wider, then the dovetail joint can be concealed.

The dovetail marking gauge defines the sides to the sockets on the bottom of the rail.

Where, for example, a thicker leg is being connected to a thinner rail, the dovetail connection can be concealed internally, and again a tapered connection makes assembly easier.

A description of preparing a tapered dovetail bridle joint should provide sufficient detail for you to prepare any of these variations. In view of its most common use, I shall refer to the top of the 'T' as the rail, and the vertical of the 'T' as the leg.

## Initial Stock Preparation

For this variation, the parts are prepared the same thickness, and squared all round. For the concealed variations the leg should be at least 6mm (1/4in) thicker than the rail, allowing a 3mm (1/8in) cover each side. Much less and this will be too fragile in most common woods to survive the process.

## Marking Out and Cutting

Proceed with marking out as for a common bridle joint, marking the width of the leg on to the bottom edge of the rail, and the width of the rail down from the top of the leg, carrying this marking right round the top. Using a mortise gauge set to thirds, mark across the top and down the edges of the leg, and along the bottom edge of the rail, between the width marks.

Now use a dovetail marking gauge to lay in the bottom of the two sockets on the rail, taking the slope right from the intersections of the squared lines and the mortise lines.

A bevel gauge is then used to mark in the taper lines on the sides of the rail, and these are then carried across the top with the dovetail marking gauge.

The mortise gauge then connects these lines on the top of the rail to define the top of the sockets, and the waste is clearly marked.

The bottom of the tapers on the rail are used to mark the shoulders on the leg, before they are carried up to the top.

The dovetail marking gauge is used to complete marking the tails on the end of the leg, ready for sawing.

The socket sides are sawn on the rail, and the waste chopped and pared. Be sure to clean right into the corners.

After sawing the centre section out of the leg, the tapered sides of the tails are cut and fitted to the rail sockets.

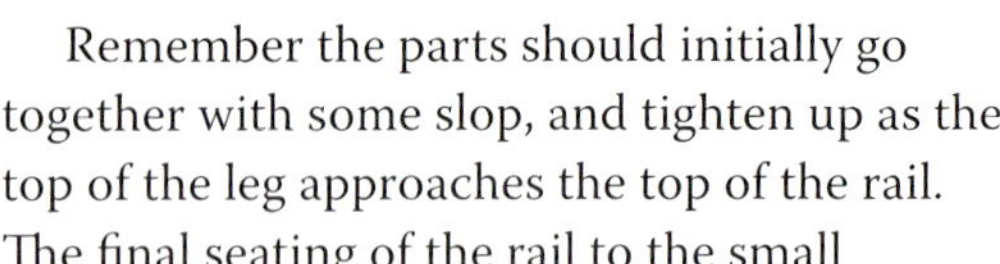

Remember the parts should initially go together with some slop, and tighten up as the top of the leg approaches the top of the rail. The final seating of the rail to the small

After the rear of the sockets is defined with the mortise gauge, all the waste can be marked before cutting begins.

Tapers are scribed up the sides of the rail using a bevel gauge. These tapers will make assembly much easier, especially when glue is used.

The shoulders on the leg can be taken directly from the rail, as can the top width of the tails.

The sides of the sockets at the top of the rail are scribed from the ends of the tapers, remembering that they should flare out towards the centre.

Once the tapers are marked in, the sloped sides of the tails are marked with a dovetail marking gauge. Notice that the tails don't extend to the edges because of the tapers.

The tapered tails are prepared last and fitted to the sockets, which is much easier than the other way around.

A double-dovetail halving, which overcomes the weaknesses inherent in edge halving joints.

After a tap with a mallet, the joint, which initially assembles easily, tightens right up.

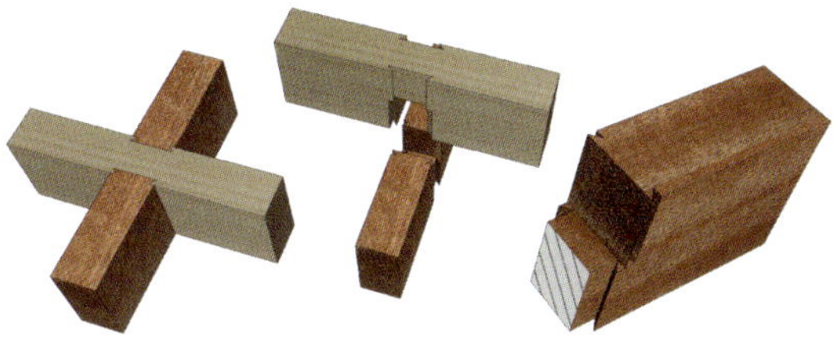

Exploded and section views of a double-dovetail halving joint, showing the complexity involved.

shoulders of the leg should need a tap of the mallet, and the joint should lock tight.

## THE DOUBLE-DOVETAIL HALVING

The double-dovetail halving, due to its much longer preparation time, is only used in place of an edge halving when the joint will be subjected to significant stresses. The dovetailed sections mechanically lock the ends within the joint from moving in any direction, which could lead to failures due to the material removed to create the halving.

The demonstration joint is of a scale that might be used to join cross-stretchers on a tea table, with the parts being shaped after the joint has been prepared.

### Initial Stock Preparation

Both parts are prepared square and true, and to the same thickness, so that the joint will be flush top and bottom. They need not be the same width, but they are for this demonstration.

### Marking Out and Cutting

The width of each part is directly knifed across the other, in the location where the joint will be made, and the knife lines squared right round. Inside both of these knife lines, on the top and bottom edges, a further two lines are knifed in, about one-eighth to one-tenth of the width of the parts (or of the smallest part if they are different widths). The same distance is gauged in from both sides as well, and a mitre square used to define the dovetails and sockets, as shown below.

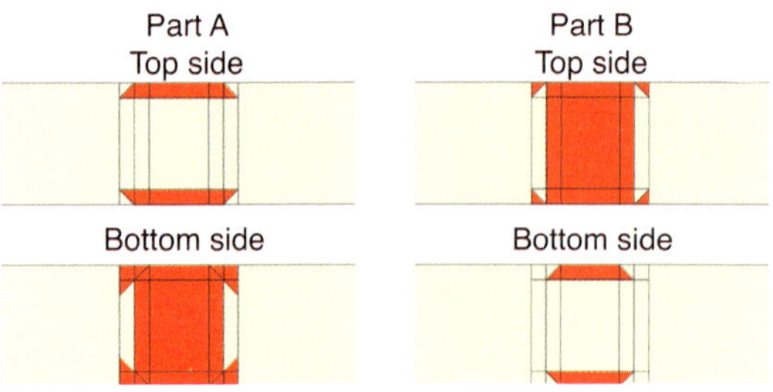


Views from the top and bottom of each part, showing (in red) the waste area that must be removed to half depth.

Gauging the centre of the depth, where the layouts change and the halving is cut.

The thickness of the parts is halved and gauged across both sides of the joint area, from the face edge on each part. Keep the gauge set as this marking will need to be re-established once some areas of waste are removed.

Clearly identify the waste to be removed before cutting. With so many knife lines it is all too easy to make a mistake, so double check.

Start by cutting in the sides and paring the sockets and tails, before cutting out the main halving sections.

The tips of the tails are quite fragile due to the 45-degree angle they are cut at, so it is best to avoid multiple dry fittings.

Accurate marking out and cutting should guarantee a good fit, although with glue it will be a hard assembly.

All the waste is clearly marked and double checked before any cuts begin.

Leaving the main halving cut until the tails and sockets are worked as much as possible.

With the main halving cut, the joint is ready to assemble. Test fitting, if tried, should be handled carefully as the corners of the tails are quite fragile and easily torn off.

The double-dovetail halving is complete, with one part stained to highlight the joint.

## THE DOVETAILED HOUSING

When a wide panel may have a tendency to cup, or the sides of a carcass might tend to spread apart, a dovetailed housing can be used to prevent this happening.

A dovetail cleat of sufficient stiffness, housed across a panel within a matching dovetailed trench, will resist stresses that could otherwise cause the panel to cup. The dovetail ensures the cleat is held tightly to the panel across its entire width. For practical purposes, cleats are usually multiple or tapered, and installed from alternate directions.

The sides of tall carcasses, such as bookcases, will spread apart in the middle as the upper shelves are loaded unless these sides are held in place by one or more fixed shelves. Shelves using common housing joints rely solely on glue to hold them together, and are only suitable in light duty applications. By introducing a dovetail to the housing, a strong mechanical fixing is achieved, which allows a bookcase to support much higher loads.

Dovetailed housing joints are often found in other applications where boards or panels are joined at right angles in a tee.

To suit different situations the dovetailed housing comes in a number of varieties, and for the purpose of demonstration the preparation of the stopped and tapered half-dovetailed housing will be described. Preparation of the other varieties are easily derived from this one.

A half-dovetailed housing joint securing the top to the side of a bookcase, prior to a back panel being installed.

Installing dovetail cleats under a table-top panel. This use of a dovetail housing will help resist any cupping of the table top that might otherwise occur, for example due to changes in moisture content.

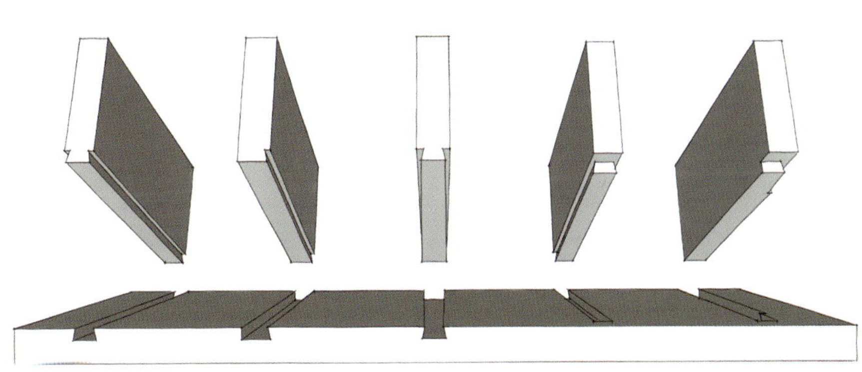

Some varieties of dovetailed housing joints. Left to right, dovetailed housing, half-dovetailed housing, tapered dovetailed housing, stopped dovetailed housing, and stopped tapered half-dovetailed and housed joints.

## The Stopped and Tapered Half-Dovetailed Housing

### Initial Stock Preparation

The panel to receive the housing (the housing panel, receiving the socket) should be prepared with a flat surface where the joint is to be made. In most cases this panel will also be thicknessed and have its ends and edges shot square.

The panel being housed (the housed panel, on to which the tail will be formed) should be thicknessed, and the joining end shot square to the face side. In most cases the joining end, or ends, will also be square to the edges.

In the case of carcasses, such as a bookcase, if a back is to be set into a rebate on the rear of the side panels, then this rebate is best prepared before housing the shelves, so that they can be aligned with the rebate.

### Marking Out and Cutting

The position of the housing is marked on the housing panel. The upper line should be knifed in for the extent of the housing, leaving a section intact from the stop position. (This stop position is the end of the housing, and prevents the joint from being visible from the front. The housed panel will end up being notched to either wholly or partly cover the stopped section.) The lower line is lightly pencilled in, and shows the maximum width to which the half-dovetailed socket should extend.

The depth of the socket, which should be approximately one-third of the housing panel thickness, is gauged at the rear of the panel between the housing marks, and the same distance gauged round the end of the housed panel.

The straight side and sloped side of the housing are marked on the rear edge of the panel. The extent of the dovetail socket must be within the thickness of the joining panel, and this throws the neck of the socket well within the previously marked pencil line.

The width of the socket opening at the rear is measured, and reduced by perhaps 10 per cent, before marking it off from the knifed line at the stop position towards the front of the housing panel. A line is now knifed to define the tapered side of the housing.

In order to facilitate sawing the housing sides, approximately 50mm (3/16in) of the housing must be chopped and pared at the stopped end. Indeed for short housings, the entire length can be prepared in this way. The dovetailed side will clearly need to be undercut too, and the dovetail marking gauge

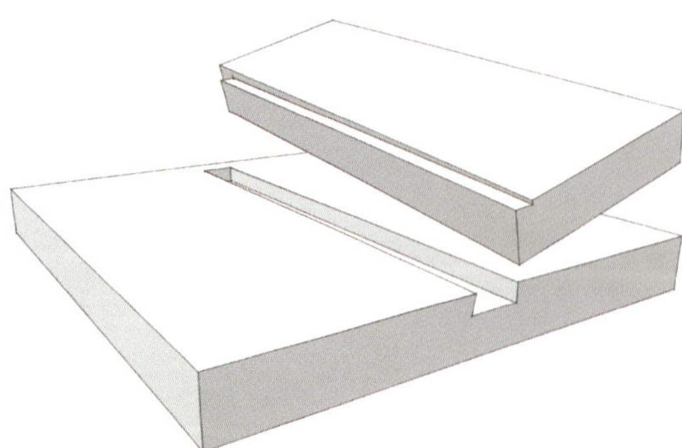
The stopped and tapered half-dovetailed housing joint: a housing joint that is easy to assemble, and resists pulling apart.

The housing panel (left) has the position of the housing pencilled in, with the straight side of the socket knifed from the rear to the stop position. The housed panel has the tail length gauged all round its end.

provides a simple jig for a chisel used to pare out this waste.

The sides of the housing are now sawn, taking care to avoid damaging the panel ahead of the stop position. The straight side of the housing will be visible as a joint line, so either leave the line and pare back to it after sawing, or create a knife wall to saw up against.

Remove the waste between the saw cuts with a chisel, and pare the bottom of the housing as smooth as possible. A router plane is ideal for this job, giving the required depth consistently and quickly.

The dovetail gauge used to mark the end of the housing is again used to jig a chisel, as the stopped end of the housing is chopped out to provide clearance to saw the remainder of the housing sides.

The end of the housing is marked in, with one side sloped and one side plumb, all within the thickness of the panel to be housed.

Sawing the dovetail side of the housing. The saw is both tilted and slightly angled to take care of the dovetail and the taper.

To create a taper to the housing, the width at the front is made smaller. However, it should not be so narrow as to compromise the strength too much.

Using a router plane to clear the waste in the housing and provide a perfect bottom at the right depth

The sawn dovetail side of the housing should now be accurately pared with a chisel, using a hardwood guide made for the purpose. Equally a side rebate plane could be used, if available, attaching a bevelled face to its depth fence.

Align the housed panel against the prepared housing, and mark in where the notch should be cut to match the stop position.

Then with the rear of the panels aligned, transfer the widest extreme of the tapered tail from the housing to the housed panel. This defines the wide end of the taper.

The narrowest width of the housing, at the stop position, is also transferred to the housed panel, and will define the neck of the tail at the notch. By using the dovetail marking gauge to lay in the correct slope, the width of the end of the tail can be found, and this defines the narrow end of the taper.

The two ends of the taper are joined with a line, the taper line, and the neck of the tail can be marked in, at both ends, to give the depth that the shoulder needs to be sawn to.

A straight hardwood batten with an edge prepared at the dovetail slope angle makes a great jig to pare the side of the housing accurately.

The maximum width of the socket is transferred to the rear of the housed panel, defining one corner of the tapered tail.

The length of the notch required is marked on the housed panel, so that it can be driven into the desired position without fouling.

The width of the narrow end of the housing, $A_1$, is transferred to the housed panel, and the dovetail slope used to determine the width for the narrow end of the tapered tail, $A_2$.

With the notch removed, the profile for the narrow end of the tapered tail can be marked in, along with the taper line from end to end, ready for cutting.

There is no sign of the half-dovetailed housing once the two panels are assembled. The joint tightens up as the parts slide together, finally locking in place due to the wedging action of the taper.

After sawing the shoulder, the side of the tail is pared from the taper line to the bottom of the saw cut.

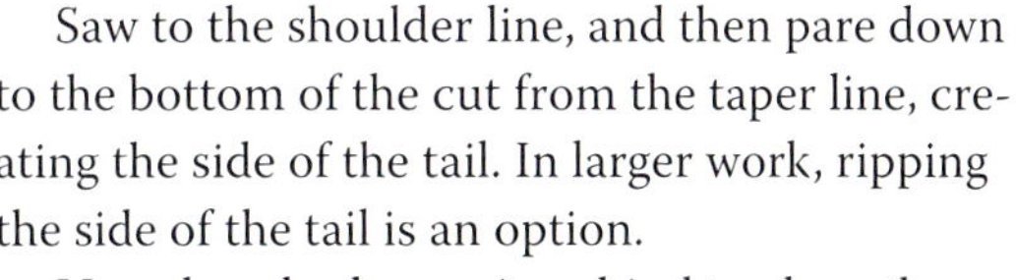

Saw to the shoulder line, and then pare down to the bottom of the cut from the taper line, creating the side of the tail. In larger work, ripping the side of the tail is an option.

Use a bevel-edge paring chisel to clean the side of the tail, and bring the joint to a good fit. A side rebate plane or shoulder plane can help, although a chisel gives the best access to the internal corner.

The joint should slide reasonably easily for about seven-eighths of the way before beginning to tighten up, and should need just a few solid blows with a mallet to finally seat it in position.

No glue should be necessary where little change in moisture content is expected, as the wedging action will lock the parts together. A little glue applied to the sloped side of the socket immediately before assembly should be all that is needed in most other circumstances.

Paring along the side of the tail to perfect the cut, and fit it to the housing.

## More Dovetailed Housings

There are three further variations I feel are worth mentioning, all of which are excellent in bookcase construction, as is the stopped and tapered half-dovetailed housing.

## The Stopped and Tapered Dovetail Housing

With a full (double-sided) dovetail, this housing can provide even more resistance to pulling apart. It is the usual variation prepared with a powered router, due to the ease and speed with which the tails and sockets can be prepared that way. However, the joint can be cut by hand using the same principles described above.

## The Stopped and Tapered Dovetailed and Housed Joints

One of these has a half dovetail, the other a full dovetail, at the front end, while the remainder of the joint is prepared as a common housing. Both resist pulling apart at the end with the dovetail, but the housed section relies fully on glue strength and should ideally be restrained by additional means, such as a fixed back panel or glue blocks.

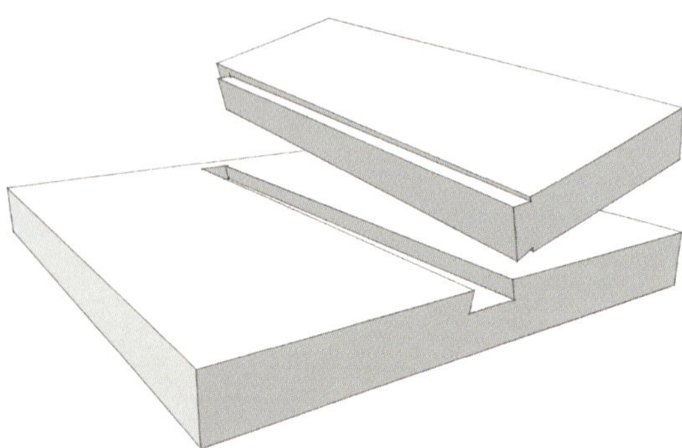

The stopped and tapered dovetailed housing joint. The full dovetail maximises this joint's resistance to pulling apart.

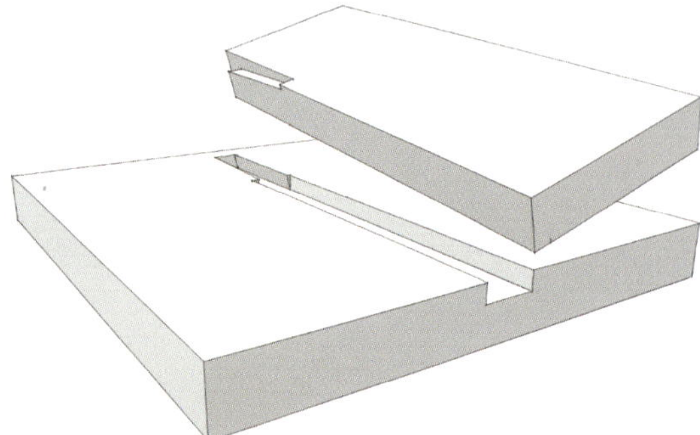

The stopped and tapered half-dovetailed and housed joint. It resists pulling apart at the dovetailed end only.

Prepared parts of a stopped and tapered dovetailed housing.

The dovetailed section can be prepared with a full dovetail, as shown here, making it a stopped and tapered dovetailed and housed joint.

## THE DOVETAIL MITRE

There are numerous ways to strengthen a mitre joint, such as a tenon and mitre joint, or dowels, but perhaps the strongest is a well fitted dovetail mitre.

Essentially this is a secret mitre dovetail with just one tail, and the thickness of the parts now greater than the width. The size of the tail relative to the parts makes it a decent challenge to prepare perfectly, and keeping the joint snug throughout fitting can be difficult.

### Initial Stock Preparation

For a standard mitre at 45 degrees, the parts should be prepared identical in width and thickness, square all round, and shot square on the ends.

### Marking Out and Cutting

The mitre cuts are first knifed in using a mitre square, or a bevel gauge set at 45 degrees. They should be marked right round, using a try-square to knife across the edges.

Accurately placing these mitre cuts is important, as a prepared tail end cannot be easily shortened due to the slope of the tail, and clearly neither part can be easily lengthened. The socket end can be shortened, and if one final length is initially in question, then the socket should be prepared on that part.

For strength, the neck of the tail should be at least one-third of the thickness of the parts being joined.

Select a suitable chisel, and set a mortise gauge to mark in the neck of the socket, and define the neck on the tail piece.

With a marking gauge and sliding bevel gauge, pencil in the sides of the socket and gauge in the length of it.

Marking out a dovetail mitre joint. The mitres have been knifed in as normal, using the mitre square, and highlighted with a sharp pencil.

A dovetail mitre looks like any normal mitre joint, but is reinforced with a hidden dovetail.

The neck of the dovetail socket will be cut with a chisel, chosen to be approximately one-third of the part's thickness. The mortise gauge has been set to mark the chisel width centrally on the part.

Marking the socket begins by gauging in the neck with the mortise gauge.

Marking in the tail on the edge of one part with a sliding bevel gauge. Transferring the layout from the socket is possible, but the depth often makes it tricky.

A bevel gauge, set to lay in the sides of the socket. The angle is chosen to give a long tail, without the flared end getting too close to the sides of the part and weakening it excessively.

Both parts of a dovetail mitre, marked out and with the waste areas defined, ready to start cutting.

Likewise, mark in the tail on the other part. With just the one tail, I prefer to mark the socket and tail this way, rather than trying to transfer the layout from one to the other, where the parts are often too long to easily position them accurately while scribing round them.

The waste to be removed should be clearly marked, as shown, before any cutting begins.

As with a secret mitre dovetail, saw as much of the sides of the socket as possible. Eventually these saw cuts will be removed when the mitre is sawn, but before that they will provide a

Sawing in the sides of the socket, as far as possible, which helps to speed up the chopping process, and provides planes from which to pare the sides into the full depth of the socket.

reference plane to pare into the far depth of the socket.

The tail sides are then sawn, without passing the mitre end or the baseline. If the marking out of the tail and socket is accurate, then sawing right up to the lines should avoid too much fitting of the joint later on.

The socket should be chopped out to full depth and length. If a mortise chisel isn't available, or the socket is particularly large, then bore out most of the waste and pare back to the lines.

Saw the mitre right across the socket end, and around the sides and end of the tail end. The socket mitre can be shot on a shooting board with a mitre fence, or else pared accurately, as the tail mitre.

Saw the excess from the end of the tail. It doesn't need to be snug against the back of the socket, and a slight gap will allow any excess glue somewhere to go.

Perform any final fitting before gluing the joint together. A pair of callipers can help identify errors in the wall thickness of the socket,

Sawing the sides of the tail, as far as possible. My experience is that sawing to the lines will inevitably leave some fitting work if I have chopped the socket accurately.

Sawing the mitre on the part with the socket. Half of the chopping work will end up in the bin, but this is my preferred method.

Chopping out the socket with a mortise chisel, which is great but not essential, as a bevel-edge chisel will do. To clean out the rear corners, a pair of skew chisels will be useful.

The cheeks of the tail are sawn off, the end is cut back to length, and the mitre is ready to clean up.

Both parts of the dovetail mitre are prepared and ready for assembly.

A puzzling looking joint, the rising dovetail is very practical in the right circumstances.

Dry fit of the dovetail mitre joint. A little extra fitting could get the mitre line more tightly closed.

Design of a sturdy workbench incorporating rising dovetails to attach the front legs to the solid top.

and also prevent removal of material from the wrong place.

Like the secret mitre dovetail, the fact that the dovetail is hidden means this joint is usually just for the purist, and other solutions are often employed. However, even if you never have a use for it, just preparing one will help hone your hand skills.

## THE RISING DOVETAIL

You might imagine from looking at it, that the rising dovetail would be classed as a puzzle joint. Certainly at first glance it can appear impossible to construct, however, this joint has a most practical application and it would be unfair to class it as simply a puzzle.

For at least a few centuries, the rising dovetail has been used to attach thick, solid tops to sturdy legs in the construction of workbenches. The main reasons for using it in situations such as this is that it tightens up during assembly, locking itself into position and reducing racking, and it allows the front of a workbench to finish flush with the legs, which is extremely practical when clamping work against the bench.

The mystery of the rising dovetail joint is explained once it is seen separated.

Using a marking gauge to mark the baseline, down from the top of the leg, after which the thickness of the shoulders will also be gauged.

For the preparation example I shall use the terms 'top' and 'leg' for the two parts, as these are almost exclusively what they will be in real world situations. The top will have the socket prepared in the front of it, and the leg will have the tail prepared on its end.

## Initial Stock Preparation

The top is thicknessed, and prepared with a straight and squared edge. The leg is prepared square in section, and with a squared end.

## Marking Out and Cutting

Accurate measuring out is essential for a good fit, since the two halves of this joint are, for the most part, independently marked out.

The thickness of the top is transferred to a marking gauge and gauged round the end of the leg, giving the tail baseline.

The thickness of the shoulders is gauged on the leg sides and end. These shoulders should be sized sufficiently to support the weight of the top. With the leg held in the vise, offer up the top and transfer the side shoulder lines, before squaring them round to the underside.

The rear shoulder is gauged on to the underside of the top, showing the position at which the dovetail will first enter during assembly.

Transferring the leg's side shoulder lines across to the top in its desired position. Directly transferring these prevents any measurement errors.

After gauging the desired dovetail thickness on the top and the leg, the sides of the dovetail are marked using a sliding bevel gauge. A slope of one-in-three or one-in-four works well.

On the underside of the top, the same slope angle is used to join the meeting points of the rear shoulder line and side shoulder lines to the front edge. The dovetail this creates, matches the previous one at its widest end, and will allow the tail to enter.

The dovetails marked on the top and underside are joined across the front edge, completing the socket layout.

Marking in the sloped sides of the socket opening on the upper side of the top. The same slope will be used to mark the underside of the socket but will be offset as the tail enters the top, back from the front edge.

Marking in the slope that connects the exposed tail at the top to the rear shoulder. The slopes of the front tail are taken from the front of the socket, after connecting the upper and underside marking-out lines.

The socket is defined and the waste marked out on the front and underside of the top.

The finished socket after chopping out the waste and paring smooth the sides and clean corners.

The sliding bevel gauge is set to the slope of the dovetail now created on the top's front edge, and used to lay out the dovetail on the front of the leg. Complete the marking out of the leg by joining the rear line of the dovetail on the end, to the intersection of the shoulders towards the rear of the leg.

Start with sawing the socket. Cut the sides, following the three slope lines, down to the rear of the dovetails marked on the topside and underside. An additional cut through the middle will ease removal of the waste. Chop out the waste material from the socket, and complete

Sawing the back slope on the tail after the sides have been cut, but before removing the sides with a shoulder cut.

Smoothing the rear slope of the tail. The rear shoulder prevents a bench plane from completing this, so a shoulder plane, or even a paring chisel, should be used.

The prepared tail on the end of the leg. The neck that will show is quite narrow, but overall it is quite substantial.

The completed rising dovetail joint, unglued, but very difficult to take apart.

by using a paring chisel to create a smooth flat slope, with both corners cleaned out.

Saw to the dovetail lines on the top and front of the leg. Leave the shoulder cuts to allow the back slope to be cut next, following the marked lines.

Saw the rear shoulder releasing the rear waste, and use a shoulder plane to clean the rear slope.

Cut away the remaining waste at the side shoulders, to reveal the completed tail.

## THE DOVETAIL TENON

The dovetail tenon provides a 'knock-down' equivalent to the stub mortise-and-tenon joint. The dovetail element holds the tenon in place, unless forced in one particular direction, which then allows the tenon to be withdrawn.

The simplest version, when assembled, shows the mortise into which the dovetail-shaped tenon was first inserted, and peering inside the mortise reveals the dovetail secret.

To hide the entrance, the tail can be formed on just one half or less of the tailboard.

A dovetail tenon, looking just like a stub mortise and tenon joint.

A standard dovetail tenon requires a mortise twice as long as the connecting piece is wide, and consequently when assembled half of the mortise is open to view.

The mortise can be reduced in length accordingly, and the extra-large shoulder of the tailboard ends up covering the entrance half of it. Preparation of this secret dovetail tenon is described here.

## Initial Stock Preparation

In most cases parts are prepared square and true, and the tailboard is shot square at the end. However, like mortise-and-tenon joints, the parts don't necessarily have to be square, or joined at a right angle.

## Marking Out and Cutting

A mortise and tenon are marked out on the parts in the normal way, and then a narrower waist defined for the dovetail side of both.

The mortise is first chopped with one end narrower than the other, before flaring the sides towards the back of the mortise to create a dovetail socket within the mortise. After that, the tail is sawn, ensuring that it is left a little oversize so that it can be pared to a tight fit.

The end of the tail should be tight entering the full-width half of the mortise, and only slide into the socket when its shoulders are tight up against the face around the mortise.

To preserve strength, the tail should be prepared such that its waist is one-third the thickness of the board, and its height is a full half of the board's width. A well produced joint like this will require close inspection to notice there is no edge shoulder at the tail side, and that the mortise opening is the full width of the tailboard.

Marking out is similar to a mortise and tenon, just with some additional lines.

Here the tail is half the width of the piece, so the entry hole will just be blinded when assembled.

The tail enters the normal end of the mortise to begin assembly.

Dovetail key bridging a natural split in a board. In this application the dovetail key is commonly known as a 'bow tie' or 'Dutchman'.

When fully inserted in the normal end of the mortise, the tail aligns with the dovetail socket and can be slid into place, after which the blind dovetail tenon hides its complexity.

A dovetail key used to join two boards. The key is cut first, then knifed round in place and the two sockets cut.

## DOVETAIL KEYS

Just as two pieces can be dovetailed together by preparing a socket on one and a tail on the other, so three pieces can be joined by creating a socket on two and a double-ended tail. These double-ended tails are known as dovetail keys, or dovetail splines in cases when they are thicker than they are wide.

There are good reasons to consider what sounds like more work. The grain orientation may not suit preparing tails perpendicular to the joint, for example when joining two long-grain edges together, or mitring pieces. When joining softwoods, a hardwood key is less likely to deform and fail than a tail prepared on one of the other pieces. It can also be used purely for decoration or to patch over a defect.

A dovetail key used as a spline to join two boards on a mitre joint. The end grain of the key should face the mitred ends of the joint for maximum strength.

Another frequent use of dovetail keys is to stabilise a crack running through a board, where one or more keys are installed across the crack.

## Initial Stock Preparation

The material from which the keys are to be cut should be thicknessed oversize in relation to the sockets it will be used in. This allows for trimming back and planing flush, which will remove any dents made during installation.

The surfaces into which the keys will be installed can be flattened, which will make the transfer of layout and the preparation of sockets easier.

## Marking Out and Cutting

The keys are prepared first, and so long as good practice is adhered to with regard to the slope of the tails, they can be marked out by eye with a ruler and pencil. They don't need to be symmetrical, but keeping to straight lines will make preparing the joint easier.

Most keys can be cut in the same way as cutting tails on the end of a board, and just flipping the stock over in the vise to complete the other half. Longer keys, dovetail splines, are much easier to cut on a table saw or router table, but can be cut by hand at the bench. The waist can be sawn in, the sides pared down to the base of the cut, and a shoulder plane used to true the sloped sides.

The keys and sockets can be prepared with a slight taper to their sides, in the hope that they tighten up as the keys are driven home. But I prefer to prepare both with plumb sides, and add a tiny chamfer to the entry side of the key to aid entry. Either way, a tight-fitting key will look and perform better than a sloppy one.

Dovetail keys cut by hand, and with a powered router using a template.

For stabilising cracks such as this one, use different-sized keys according to the gap for a better aesthetic.

Dovetail keys used for function and effect in a live edge, waterfall side table I made in very characterful English oak.

## THE MECHANICS OF WOODEN DOVETAILS: PART 3

### Glue Effect on Strength

By using glue on the long-grain to long-grain joint surfaces, the dovetail joint can be locked in its assembled state. The direction in which it was assembled, and could therefore be taken apart, is no longer such a weak point. The rigidity afforded to the joint by the glue helps prevent the joint from walking apart over time, so carcasses and drawers remain square so long as the glue joint doesn't fail, or the tails shear.

In comparison to an unglued joint, since the tail cannot move and create the compressive force across itself, the shear strength is not increased and shear failure could occur earlier as force is applied.

The notion that glued joints are less resistant to pulling apart is quite compelling, but with evidence very limited and anecdotal, to my mind the reasoning remains a hypothesis.

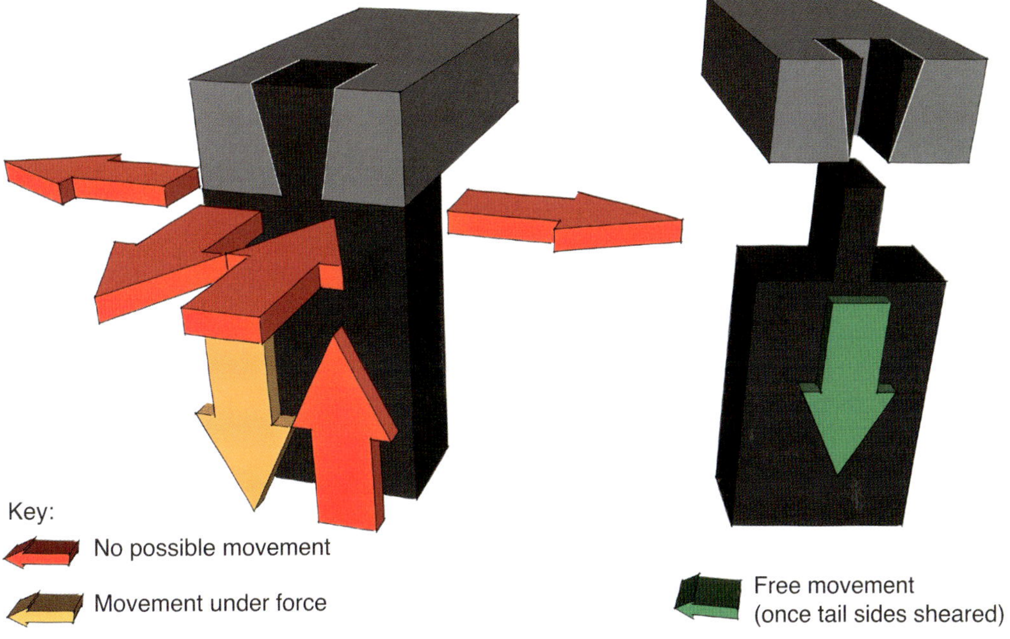


Freedom of movement and failure in glued dovetail joints.

CHAPTER 6

# PUZZLE JOINTS

Whether by nature or nurture, humans have a good instinct for spotting impossible situations. We know a square peg won't fit in a round hole whose diameter is less than the square's diagonal, just as we know a dovetail joint will only assemble if the two parts are aligned and slid together on one axis. This instinct is employed by the makers of wooden puzzles to make dovetail puzzle joints, using the fact that wood is opaque to mask the assembly secret and create an illusion.

The accuracy of the joinery is quite important in order to carry off the illusion well, especially when the observer can handle the puzzle and inspect it up close. Certainly by practising making these joints you can hone your layout and cutting skills.

The puzzle joints that follow are my first attempts, having no particular interest in them myself, and I have much respect for those who prepare them faultlessly.

The impossible bridle joint looks as if it can't be assembled due to the dovetail on one side.

## THE IMPOSSIBLE BRIDLE

Given the similarity to the rising dovetail joint described earlier, it is possible to guess how the impossible bridle is prepared: it is simply a rising dovetail joint that includes the rear half of a bridle joint. As the tail rises into position, so the back of the bridle joint comes together.

### Initial Stock Preparation

The two parts should be prepared square and true, and of equal thickness. To my mind the depth of the mortised piece should be kept close to the thickness for the illusion to work best. The end of the tenoned and dovetailed piece should be shot square.

Four impossible-looking dovetail joints, which can be made as puzzles.

## Marking Out and Cutting

The rising dovetail can be prepared in the same way as shown previously, where the sides of the dovetail socket will be flat and the slopes of the dovetail will be determined during the layout. However, for a flared dovetail, which will look more impressive, the angle for assembly would need to be too shallow to allow for the bridle joint. Therefore I choose both dovetail slopes and the assembly angle, mark out for those, and then prepare the mortise to fit and allow assembly. This is a puzzle joint, not a structural joint,

Like a rising dovetail, the impossible dovetail assembles on a diagonal.

Parts marked out for a rising dovetail and half a bridle joint, back to back.

Dry fitted, the assembled parts fit quite well, and a clamp should pull them fully home.

The prepared parts are ready for assembly. The dovetail mortise in this version has a more complicated shape in order to slope the face dovetail heavily, strengthening the optical illusion.

Glued, flush planed and oiled, the impossible dovetail is ready to confuse.

so as long as the visible joint lines are a good fit, internal gaps can be ignored.

The dovetail and tenon are sawn first, and pared to their mark-out lines. The end of the dovetail is used to lay out for the mortise on the top and bottom faces, and the dovetail marking gauge used to lay out the front of the dovetail mortise, before the connecting lines can be completed. The mortise is then sawn and chopped, and finally pared to a good fit.

The completed joint should assemble easily, tightening up as the faces align.

With the joint glued, it can be planed to flush the faces and remove all traces of layout lines, before being given a coat of finish to enhance the contrast of the woods being used.

## THE CROSSED DOUBLE DOVETAIL

A very common puzzle joint, the crossed double dovetail – or just double dovetail – is very confusing at first sight. In reality it is quite easy to prepare once cutting dovetails has been learnt.

### Initial Stock Preparation

There are two ways to prepare the joint, one is slightly easier but wastes half the overall material, the other only has waste removed around the pins and tails. For the wasteful method the stock should first be prepared square all round with sides that are the length of the finished puzzle diagonals.

The less wasteful method is described below, and the stock should be prepared square all round to the puzzle dimensions.

### Marking Out and Cutting

First a shoulder line is gauged round the ends of both parts. Tails and matching sockets are marked on the four sides of the joining ends, and diagonals used to connect them.

The waste is carefully sawn, chopped, and pared from the two sockets. Because of the angle of the sockets across the end and the slope of the socket sides, there are fragile corners that may break off in some woods.

Next the tails are prepared by sawing the sides and shoulders, and chopping and paring

In the simplest method, twin dovetails are prepared parallel between two opposite faces, and then the edge corners are planed away to reveal the finished puzzle.

The crossed double dovetail is a well known woodworking puzzle.

By cutting the dovetails on the diagonal, the crossed double dovetail can be prepared with little waste.

Sawing the socket sides with a rip panel saw to clear the long kerfs more easily.

The finished crossed double dovetail, enhanced with some finish.

Chopping the waste is taken slowly, with the part held in a vise, or cradled in a V block on the bench.

Careful paring will allow a sliding fit with tight joint lines, unless a corner has split out, as has happened here.

the waste between them. Again, be careful with the acute corners, which can be prone to breaking.

By just leaving the lines in the previous steps, the joint will be far too tight to assemble, and some judicious paring will be needed to achieve a sliding fit, which also has tight joint lines.

As with most joints, a few passes of a smoothing plane will make everything look a little cleaner, removing layout and gauge lines, and preparing the surfaces for a coat of finish.

## THE TRIPLE DOVETAIL

I had only ever seen the triple-dovetail puzzle as a drawing in Edwin Wyatt's *Wonders in Wood*, where he explains that the idea came from a magazine, *Industrial Arts and Vocational Education* (January, 1930). Writing this book was the inspiration needed to prepare the puzzle joint myself, and I had to include it here.

### Initial Stock Preparation

Looking at the finished joint, it appears that the tail section is quite thin, and that as such the socket piece, or base, need not be so thick. This is, of course, a clue to the illusion.

The triple-dovetail puzzle joint. It was seemingly impossible to construct, especially when viewed in real life, but it was genuinely possible.

An offcut of the stock allows dividers to be coplanar when used to scribe the curved sides of the socket and tail, ensuring greater accuracy.

The illusion is possible since the tail dives beneath the top surface of the socket, where there is more space, before rising back up as it reaches the other side.

The prepared stock, and a shop-made hook-dovetail marking gauge that can be used within the socket.

The tail section has a convex bottom, and the bottom of the socket is concave to match. Therefore the stock for the tail section should initially be prepared squared all round and approximately 50 per cent thicker than the exposed end grain. The base should be squared all round and at least one-third thicker than the stock for the tail.

Offcuts of each prepared piece can be helpful when scribing arcs later on, ensuring pivot point and scribe are coplanar.

## Marking Out and Cutting

Centre lines are marked on the base, and then a line offset each side of the cross-grain one, representing the narrowest dimension of the socket across the width of the base.

A pair of spring dividers, set on the long-grain centre line, are used to scribe in the waist of the socket top, and also the top of the tail piece.

The end tails are marked on the base and tail piece, and should be identical in size and shape. The slope I chose to use was 1:3, which gives a nice appearance, and clearly shows the dovetail when viewed from any angle.

The curved bottom is scribed on to the tail piece, and also on to a stiff piece of card that will aid the hollowing of the socket. The radius for this curve can be calculated, or found from full size drawings.

The marking out for the socket is complete and ready for cutting.

Initial clearing of the socket by sawing and chopping, until the bottom is flat.

Scribing the layout lines for the tail to match those of the socket.

Using a template cut to the radius for the bottom of the socket, to help shape it correctly.

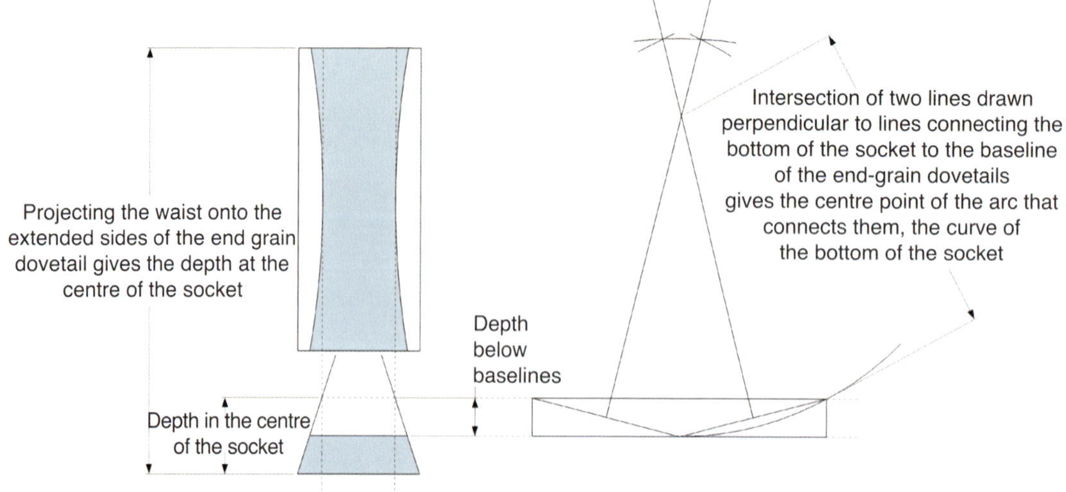



Using drafting to find the depth of the socket in the centre, and the radius for the curve for the bottom of the socket.

Initially the waste is removed from one side to the other, maintaining the sloped sides while following the curved top profile.

Then the concave bottom can be excavated using the card template for guidance, and extending the sloped sides to meet it.

The bottom of the tail piece is rounded to the same curve, initially by sawing, then rasping, and finally planing.

Removing the waste between the bottom curved edge and the curves on the top of the tail piece is done with a rounded spokeshave, or rasps and files, until the pieces slide together.

Wyatt describes adding a loose-fitting plug within the joint, such that it locks when upright, and releases when held upside down.

Planing the curve on the bottom of the tail to match the socket bottom: the first step in fitting the joint.

Almost there, as the socket and tail close to a perfect match.

Using a spokeshave to create the complex side bevel on the tail, checking frequently with the dovetail gauge, and eventually creating a sliding fit in the socket.

The finished triple-dovetail puzzle, with the contrast enhanced by the application of some mineral oil.

## THE TWIN RISING DOVETAIL

The twin rising dovetail is the odd one out in the four puzzle joints that I have included, since it relies on the flexibility of the wood rather than the direction of assembly. The resulting joint has little strength and no practical purpose, however it still proves to be good practice for hand skills.

A very similar puzzle joint, the double double dovetail, is slightly easier to make but even weaker, lacking any long-grain to long-grain glue surfaces.

### Initial Stock Preparation

Both parts are prepared square and true, and to the same thickness. The material chosen for the sockets, forming the crossbar in this example, should be chosen for its bending ability, which may give away the trick to this particular puzzle joint.

In this example I have chosen English ash, which is very commonly used for bent work.

### Marking Out and Cutting

Two rising dovetail-shaped tails are marked out on opposite faces at the end of the upright, although they have no sloped rear. The crossbar is marked out for the corresponding sockets. Essentially the layout is very like a dovetail-shaped bridle joint.

The waste is removed from the sides of the tails, leaving the middle of the piece intact, except for a groove between the tails at the end. This groove should be shallow at each end, but curve down to the centre. The reason for that will become clear when the joint is assembled.

Next the dovetail sockets are sawn and cleaned of waste. The back bevels of the sockets should all be completed whilst the central web is left complete and the piece is still strong.

Taking extreme care, the central web of the crossbar is now sawn and pared away, leaving

Both parts marked out for preparing a twin rising-dovetail puzzle joint. There is similarity with a bridle joint at this point.

The twin rising dovetail. It takes a little trickery to get this puzzle joint together. It is useful to choose a wood that bends well for the crossbar if you decide to try this joint.

The tails are exposed and a groove is being pared through the middle to accept the spine of the crossbar.

just a thin long-grain attachment at the top. This will partly fill the groove in the top of the upright, and give the impression that it carries right through. Tapered grooves in the sides of the socket will accept the webbing left on each side of the upright.

Final fit will no doubt require a little fettling, and in order to test assembly the thin spine left on the crossbar should be either steamed or soaked with hot water to make it flexible.

Once fitted, a little pressure applied to straighten the crossbar should bring the socket sides tight round the tails.

The twin rising dovetail with its integral webs has enough good glue surface area to hold it together under scrutiny, and it should definitely be glued to avoid the thin spine breaking.

Ready to assemble, the complexity can clearly be seen. The crossbar is now quite delicate, and should be handled carefully.

A well fitted twin rising dovetail will spring partially open unless pressure is applied or the joint glued.

With the spine moistened in hot water, it can be flexed enough to assemble the joint. When flexed, the spine needs extra depth in the centre of the groove.

Allow plenty of time for the moistened joint to dry after gluing, before cleaning up with a smoother and applying some finish. Then baffle your friends with it

CHAPTER 7

# MAKING A DOVETAIL BOX

There are countless ways of using the dovetail knowledge that you will accumulate through reading this book and working through the joints. This chapter describes a small project that will put some of this new-found knowledge into practice.

## DESIGN

The main carcass is a simple rectangle, split through the centre to make two identical compartments. There is a continuous grain pattern round the outside, and the corners are through-dovetailed. The divider is dovetail housed into the inside, front and rear of the box. The base is captured within a groove cut into the inside faces of all the sides (the groove being stopped on the two sides where it would come through the joint otherwise).

In a break from dovetailing, the lid uses a simple knuckle joint, which allows either compartment to be accessed independently. Of course a simple lift-off lid, or a pair of lids, would make an equally functional box.

American cherry was chosen for its workability and lovely colour, which is enhanced with two applications of boiled linseed, both wiped off and allowed to dry; three coats of blonde shellac are then applied with a polishing rubber.

## CUTTING LIST AND MATERIALS

All the wood that is needed is given in the cutting list. The plywood can be swapped for MDF if required, or solid wood if some allowance for expansion and contraction is made by reducing the dimension across the grain.

Sawing all the solid parts from a single board should help maintain a good colour match, and by starting with a thick enough piece from which to resaw all the pieces, it should be possible to achieve the continuous grain match around the box, and a pair of book-matched lids.

To fit out the inside of the box for jewellery, some foam and baize are ideal, and can be either dry fitted or stuck in place with glue.

In addition you will require a hinge pin, if you are making the swinging lids. A mirror screw with a wide cover is ideal, and the holes in the box should be sized to the screw.

Twin swivelling lids cover two compartments in this dressing-table box with through and housing dovetail joints.

| Part(s) | Material | Qty | Length (mm) | Width (mm) | Thickness (mm) |
|---|---|---|---|---|---|
| Front | Hardwood | 1 | 170 | 50 | 10 |
| Rear | Hardwood | 1 | 170 | 50 | 10 |
| Sides | Hardwood | 2 | 129 | 50 | 10 |
| Divider | Hardwood | 1 | 117 | 40 | 10 |
| Tops | Hardwood | 2 | 129 | 104 | 10 |
| Bottom | Plywood | 1 | 158 | 117 | 6 |

(All dimensions are of finished parts. Add 2mm for rough cutting length and width.)

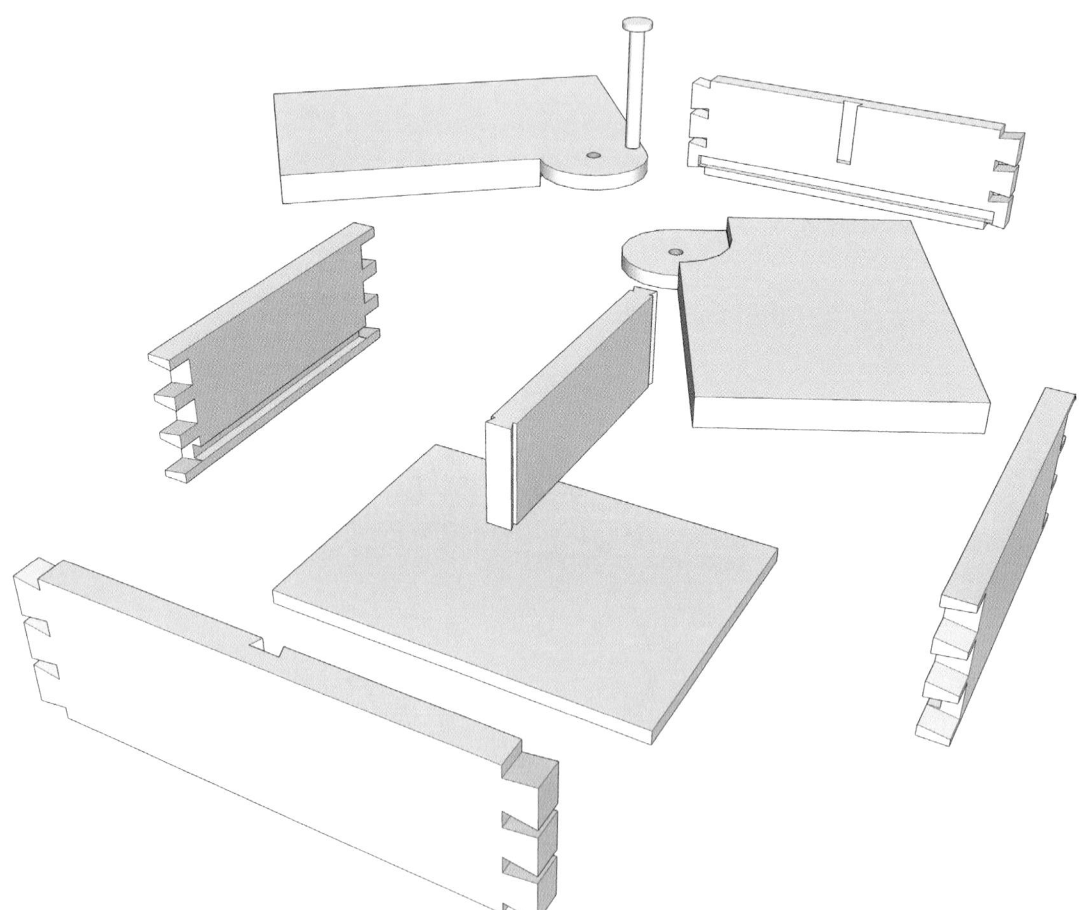

Exploded diagram of the twin swivel-lid dovetailed box.

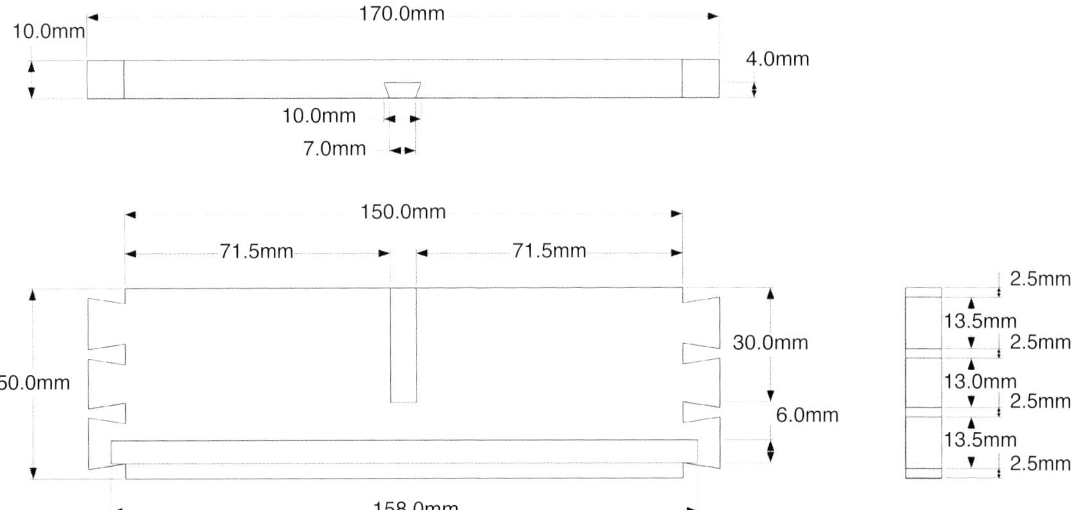


Identical front and rear sides, with suggested dimensions and tail layout.

Identical left and right sides, with suggested dimensions and pin layout.

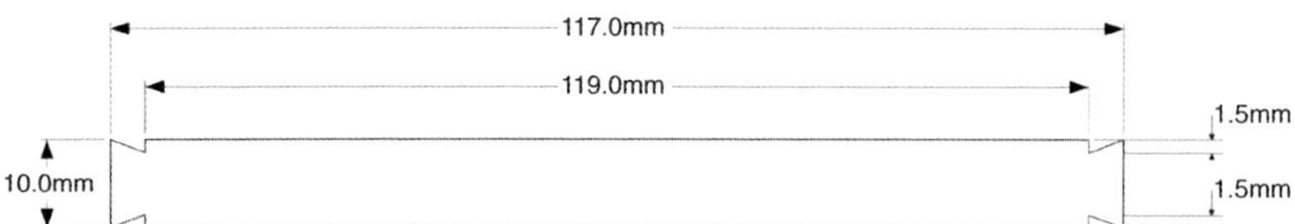

Central divider with sliding dovetail ends, and suggested dimensions.

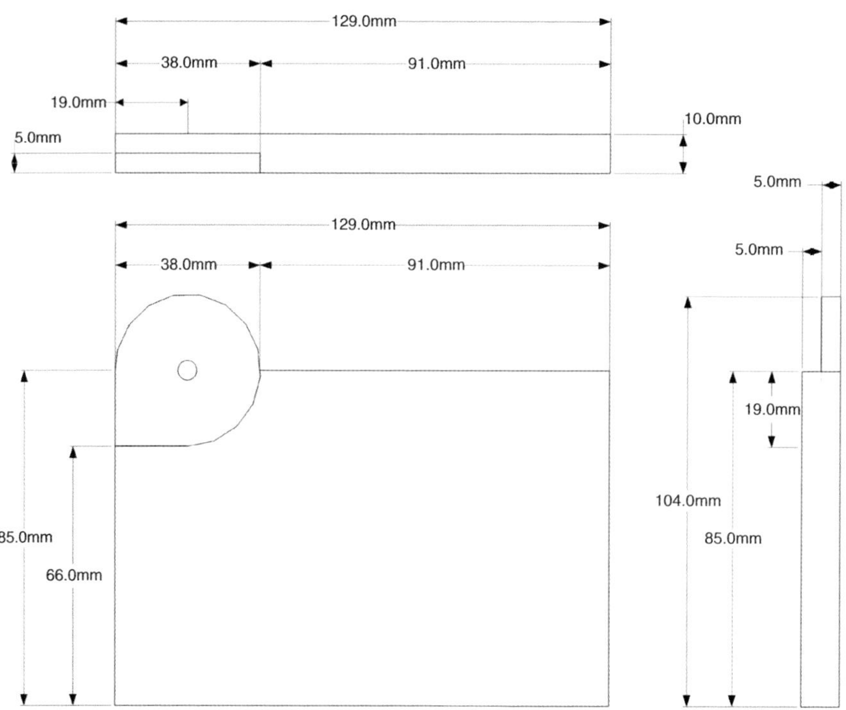


Identical left and right lids. One is flipped over to allow them to mate and the knuckle joint to function.

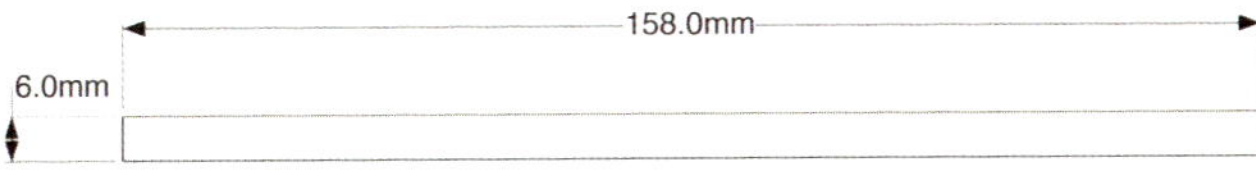

Plain panel bottom, with suggested dimensions for MDF or ply. For solid wood, the width should be reduced to allow for expansion.

## ORDER OF WORK

### Separating the Pieces

Start by breaking down the board into the pieces in the cutting list, leaving them all a little oversize.

If you are starting with a thick board that needs resawing, the two lids should be resawn together, and the pieces to make up the carcass should be resawn from a piece that is a little longer than the front and one side. Going from one end, the front should be facing a side, and the other side should be facing the back. It sounds complicated, but essentially the outside faces of the carcass all unwrap from the resawn surfaces, which means that the front and side, and side and rear, must be left attached until after the board is resawn.

After resawing, leave the pieces overnight to settle, as they will most likely cup or wind a little as the internal stresses balance out. Flatten the pieces on one side, then thickness them, and shoot the edges and ends square, and to final dimensions.

All the parts can be cut from a small board, in this case American cherry, ensuring a good colour match in the finished box. At this stage, each piece cut will later be resawn to yield two or more identical or similar parts.

### Preparing the Swivel Lids

The one exception is that of the two lid halves, which should be thicknessed but left oversize until the hinge knuckles are prepared and the two halves can be assembled on top of the glued-up carcass. By shooting these to size last, a perfect alignment can be achieved, even if the carcass isn't quite to size.

Pick a forstner bit as close to the design size for the knuckle as you have available, and use this as the actual size. Locate for the centre points on the two lid halves and bore halfway through, from the top of one half, and from the bottom of the other.

Saw away most of the excess material from the knuckle and carefully pare back to the layout lines. A hand screw clamped to the lid will provide a square reference from which clean-up shavings can be taken with the chisel.

A forstner bit removes half of the thickness of the lid where the knuckle joint will be created.

The four sides of the carcass are laid out on a single piece of the board, which will be sawn so there is a continuous grain pattern round the box.

Using a small cherry frame saw with a coping blade, to cut the waste away from the knuckle joint in one of the cherry swivel lids.

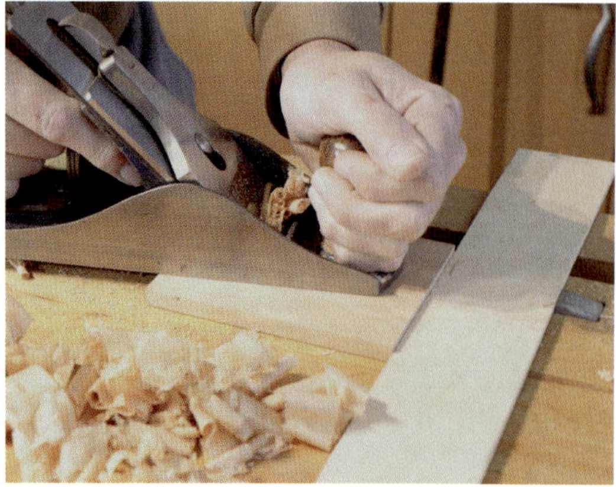

Resawn pieces for the swivel lids are flattened, thicknessed and smoothed after resawing from the rough board.

Taking smoothing cuts with a paring chisel, up to the knuckle on one of the lids. The hand-screw jaws can be precisely lined up to guide the chisel accurately.

The two lids should swivel smoothly at the knuckle, before the hole for the hinge pin is bored through.

Gang cutting the tails on the front and rear sides of the carcass. Alternatively the tails could be cut on the left and right sides, depending on your preference.

Pare or file the round of the knuckle until the surface left by the forstner bit is just revealed from the edge, then fettle the joint until the two halves interlock and rotate cleanly. The final pivot hole can be bored through for the mirror screw hinge pin.

## Preparing the Carcass

Lay out for the through dovetails in the normal way, ganging the front and rear pieces to speed up the process and help accuracy. If two or four tails are your preference, then divide up the boards accordingly.

Saw all the tails and clean up with a chisel before transferring the layout to the sides, which will be prepared with matching pins. If you've practised the corner joints in Chapter 4 then you should soon have the pins cut and these four pieces fitting well together.

To accommodate the bottom panel in the carcass, cut a groove into all four pieces. The pinboards can have the groove running end to end, since the end of the groove will be covered by a tail, however the tailboard grooves must be stopped short of the ends to prevent them showing on the finished box.

A divider is prepared with a housing dovetail at each end that will slide into housings in the front and rear of the carcass. This is a nice touch, but not at all necessary in

Using a small plough plane to run the groove for the bottom panel of the box in one of the sides. Stopped grooves are needed in the front and rear to prevent them showing on the assembled box.

Sides and divider parts almost complete, with just the dovetail housing slots left to cut.

such a box, and just a reminder of the joints in Chapter 5.

With the carcass sides and divider prepared, their inside surfaces should be polished in shellac or lacquer, which is much easier to do while they are separate. Then the MDF bottom can be sized to fit, and the whole assembly glued up. Covering the bottom panel in baize or veneer is an option here, depending on the intended use.

## Finishing Off

Flush off all the carcass joints, and ease all the edges with a block plane or sandpaper. Polish the external surfaces with boiled linseed oil followed by shellac or lacquer.

Position the swivel lids on the carcass and mark the position of the hinge pin in the divider, then bore a pilot hole for it. With the lids attached, the excess width and length are marked, before removing and shooting them to the precise size.

A chamfer on the edges of the lids gives a nice feeling when opening and closing, and finishes off the woodworking. They are polished in the same way as the carcass, and attached with a very thin plastic washer in the knuckle joint. A small stop can be glued on the underside of each lid to prevent it swinging beyond the divider, and the screw tightened to give just the right amount of friction.

Not strictly required, the dovetail housed joint for the central divider will keep the corners pulled together if later on the glue fails in them.

Lids swivel on a simple mirror fixing screw, which is tightened to give suitable friction to its operation.

The joints are carefully planed flush, ensuring that the upper edges are all in plane with each other so that the lids fit well.

The finished dovetailed box, fitted out to hold a wristwatch, wedding band and cufflinks.

# BIBLIOGRAPHY


Blandford, P. W., *The Illustrated Handbook of Woodworking Joints* (Tab Books Inc., 1984).

Hayward, C. H., *Woodwork Joints* (Bell & Hyman Ltd, 1984).

Joyce, E., *Encyclopedia of Furniture Making* (Sterling Publishing Co. Inc., 1987).

Kingshott, J., *A Woodworker's Guide to Joints* (B. T. Batsford Ltd, 1998).

Laughton, R., *Success with Joints* (Guild of Master Craftsmen Publications Ltd, 2005).

Ross, R. J., *Wood Handbook – Wood as an Engineering Material*. General technical report. FPL-GTR-282. (Madison, WI: US Department of Agriculture, Forest Service, Forest Products Laboratory, 2021).

Walker, K. S., Gorman, J., and Lear, K., 'The Relationship Between Dovetail Angle and Joint Strength', *Woodworker Magazine* (January 1958).

Wyatt, E. M., *Wonders in Wood* (Stobart Davies, 1997).

Wooden scrub plane with dovetailed sole made by the author.

Sunrise 'dovetail'. Not a true dovetail… or is it?

A wizened old man from Widdale,
never one to shirk or to fail.
He chopped an' he sawed,
in an ever shrinking board,
'til he finished his first dovetail.

# INDEX

First published in 2024 by
The Crowood Press Ltd
Ramsbury, Marlborough
Wiltshire SN8 2HR

**enquiries@crowood.com**
**www.crowood.com**



**British Library Cataloguing-in-Publication Data**
A catalogue record for this book is available from the British Library.

ISBN 978 0 7198 4445 4



Typeset by Chennai Publishing Services

Cover design by surichardsgraphicdesign.com
Printed and bound in India by Parksons Graphics

## DEDICATION

To Julie, who has always encouraged me, and silently tolerated the shavings that I walk into our home.

## ACKNOWLEDGEMENTS

My interest in woodwork was undoubtedly down to watching my father, Roy, and grandfather, Harry, making things such as cabin beds, beehives and furniture, whilst I was a small boy. Once old enough, their wisdom, guidance and encouragement ensured that most of my own childhood projects were successful, leading to the love of woodwork that has endured to this day. Indeed, I am very lucky that all my family has been of great support and encouragement throughout my life.

Several years ago, a chance meeting with Anthony Bailey, the then editor of *Woodworking Crafts* magazine, led to a suggestion that I might like to write for the magazine. The magazine publishers, Guild of Master Craftsmen, have continued to be most supportive, publishing articles of mine in all four of their titles. The response to my many articles over the last few years has ultimately led to this, my first book.

I am most grateful to friend and wood consultant Gervais Sawyer for his help and expert advice, and for sending me down a chariot rabbit warren.

Many thanks must also go to my fellow BenchTalk101 woodworkers: on our weekly Zoom meetings, which started during the first Covid-19 lockdown and continue to today, they help keep me just sane enough. And thanks also to those woodworkers I have met all round the world through my YouTube channel.

p.2: Coppiced sweet chestnut (*Castanea sativa*). A suitable wood for beginners to practise dovetail joinery, sweet chestnut is easy to work with edge tools, sawing, chopping and paring well.

p.4: Dovetail key stabilising a crack in a wide oak board.

p.6: Double bevel dovetails were chosen to add strength and interest to this otherwise simple fruit bowl made from Scots pine (*Pinus sylvestris*).

p.8: Small dovetails are appropriate in thin material such as this trinket box and model for a larger cabinet.